NAFTA

as a Model of Development:

The Benefits and Costs of Merging High and Low Wage Areas

Richard S. Belous
Jonathan Lemco
Editors

NAFTA as a Model of Development: The Benefits and Costs of Merging High and Low Wage Areas

NPA Rcport #266

Price $15.00

ISBN 0-89068-120-1
Library of Congress
Catalog Card Number 93-84765

A voluntary association incorporated under the laws
of the District of Columbia
1424 16th Street, N.W., Suite 700
Washington, D.C. 20036

Printed in the United States of America

Contents

**NAFTA as a Model of Development:
The Benefits and Costs of Merging
High and Low Wage Areas**

Richard S. Belous and Jonathan Lemco
Editors

Foreword

If the North American Free Trade Agreement is ratified, it will signal a critical turning point in North American economic integration. Bringing two modernized and wealthy nations into a close partnership with a developing country, with its many ramifications, may well set precedents for other areas of the Americas. In this regard, the NAFTA may be a model to the world.

The authors of this volume present a variety of views from different countries. Most of the authors offer policy prescriptions, and all present carefully argued cases. The views expressed in this volume are based on presentations given at a conference that was held at the Institute of the Americas in La Jolla, California, on December 14-15, 1992. The Conference, which focused on the implications of the NAFTA for developing countries, was jointly sponsored by the Friedrich Ebert Foundation, the Institute of the Americas, and the National Planning Association. The articles represent the views of the authors and not necessarily the sponsoring organizations. We agree, however, that the ideas expressed here are of vital interest and worthy of careful examination.

Malcolm R. Lovell, Jr.
President and CEO
National Planning Association

Dieter Dettke
Executive Director
Friedrich Ebert Foundation

Paul H. Boeker
President
Institute of the Americas

Acknowledgments

We would like to thank Sheila Cavanagh, Melinda Fancher, Emily Richardson, and Carola Weil for all of their help with this study. We are particularly indebted to the Friedrich Ebert Foundation and Dieter Dettke, the Executive Director of its Washington office, for supporting and encouraging this project.

About the Editors

Richard S. Belous is Vice President, International Programs, and Chief Economist at the National Planning Association, Washington, D.C. Dr. Belous is also an Adjunct Professor at the George Washington University. Before coming to NPA, he was an economist with the Conference Board and the Congressional Research Service. He was also Executive Director of the National Council on Employment Policy. His primary areas of research interest include international economics and human resources, and he has written or edited 12 books and numerous articles. Dr. Belous has been an advisor to two presidential commissions.

Jonathan Lemco is U.S. Research Director of the Canadian-American Committee and a Senior Fellow at the National Planning Association, Washington, D.C. Dr. Lemco is also the Managing Editor of *North American Outlook* and an Adjunct Professor at the Johns Hopkins University. He has written or edited 10 books and numerous scholarly articles on topics such as the implications of the NAFTA, the costs and benefits of health care reform in the United States, energy and environmental policymaking, Canadian and U.S. policy interests in Central America, and the implications of Quebec's sovereignty movement for Canada and the United States.

About the Authors

Adolfo Aguilar Zinser is Professor, Center of the United States of America, National University of Mexico.

Rudolf M. Buitelaar is Economic Affairs Officer, Division of Production, Productivity and Management, United Nations Economic Commission for Latin America and the Caribbean.

Jorge Bustamante is Professor of Sociology, Colegio de la Frontera del Norte, Tijuana, Baja California, Mexico; and Professor of Sociology, University of Notre Dame.

Isaac Cohen is Executive Director, Washington Office, United Nations Economic Commission for Latin America and the Caribbean.

Juan de Nigris is International Studies Manager, Foreign Trade Division, VITRO, Mexico.

Gustavo del Castillo V. is Chair, Department of North American Studies, El Colegio de la Frontera Norte, Tijuana, Baja California, Mexico.

William C. Doherty is Executive Director, American Institute for Free Labor Development, AFL-CIO.

Joseph Grunwald is Adjunct Professor, Graduate School of International Relations and Pacific Studies, University of California, San Diego.

Reiner Hoffmann is Director, Division for the Advancement of Research, Hans-Böckler-Stiftung, Düsseldorf, Germany.

Clark W. Reynolds is Director, Americas Program, and Professor of Economics, Stanford University.

Richard Rothstein is Research Associate, Economic Policy Institute, Washington, D.C.

Harley Shaiken is Professor of Industrial Relations, University of California, San Diego.

Daniel Szabo is Senior Advisor to the Manager, Economic and Social Development Department, Inter-American Development Bank, Washington, D.C.

John D. Tessier is Senior Management Advisor, IBM Latin America.

Cathryn L. Thorup is Acting Director, Center for U.S.-Mexican Studies, University of California, San Diego.

Sidney Weintraub is Dean Rusk Professor, LBJ School of Public Affairs, University of Texas at Austin.

Ann Weston is Director, Trade and Adjustment Program, North-South Institute, Ottawa, Canada.

Van R. Whiting, Jr., is Senior Research Fellow, Center for U.S.-Mexican Studies, and Research Associate, Graduate School of International Relations and Pacific Studies, University of California, San Diego.

Ronald Wonnacott is Professor, Department of Economics, University of Western Ontario.

Eugene W. Zeltmann is Manager of Trade and Industry Associations, GE Industrial and Power Systems, General Electric Company.

PART I

SETTING THE STAGE

1. The NAFTA Development Model of Combining High and Low Wage Areas: An Introduction

by Richard S. Belous and Jonathan Lemco

Regional trading blocs are a growing force in the global economy, and many analysts have commented on the emergence of three key regional trading zones. In North America—with or without the North American Free Trade Agreement (NAFTA)—a process of regional economic integration is taking place. Despite some setbacks, the European Community is still moving forward in the process of economic integration. Also, East Asia is experiencing increased economic linkages within that region.[1]

MIXING HIGH AND LOW WAGE AREAS

While there are many striking differences between these three emerging regional trading blocs, there is one basic feature common to each. In North America, the European Community, and East Asia, the formation of regional trading blocs involves the uniting of high and low wage areas. Figure 1 shows how large these wage differentials are. For example, in 1992, Mexican compensation rates were on average only approximately 15 percent of average compensation rates in the United States. The European Community experienced similar compensation differentials. In 1992, Portuguese compensation was on average only roughly 19 percent of German average compensation rates. Meanwhile in East Asia, the differences between Korean and Japanese compensation rates were also quite large (i.e., Korea's average compensation rate in 1992 was approximately 19 percent of average compensation paid in Japan). With China emerging as a major trading partner with many East Asian nations, Japan and other wealthy Asian countries will have to contend with very large compensation differentials created by relatively inexpensive Chinese labor.

FIGURE 1

Average Hourly Compensation Rates in Various Countries, 1992[a]
(U.S.$)

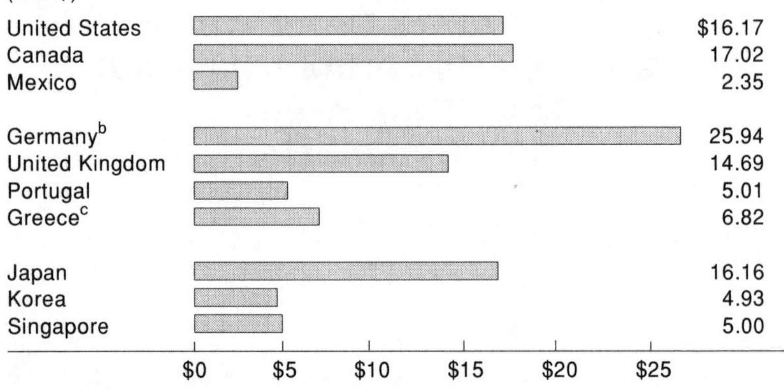

[a]Average compensation rates for manufacturing workers.

[b]Includes workers in western Germany only.

[c]1991 figure.

Source: U.S. Bureau of Labor Statistics.

Wage rates are often used as a proxy to symbolize vast labor market-related differences in various areas. As pointed out in Table 1, not only does the formation of regional trading blocs involve the linking up of markets with vastly different wage rates, but it also means blending together nations that have many different socioeconomic characteristics. While the United States in 1990 had a gross national product (GNP) per capita of almost $22,000, Mexico had a GNP per capita under $2,500 in 1990. As shown in Table 1, Canada and the United States also have experienced rates of population growth, adult literacy, life expectancy, and growth in urban populations that are different than experienced by Mexico. Similarly, Japan has numerous differences in its socioeconomic indicators compared to many of its East Asian trading partners.

Decisionmakers in government, business, labor, agriculture, and the media have been very interested in the developmental implications of creating a regional trading bloc that links high- and low-wage areas. Will such a linkage be good for both the high-wage and the low-wage areas? Will it pull down the wage rates

TABLE 1

Various Socioeconomic Indicators
(U.S.$)

	GNP per Capita, 1990	Average Annual Pop. Growth, 1980-90	Adult Illiteracy, 1990	Life Expectancy, 1990	Income Distribution % of Income Held By:		Average Annual Growth of Urban Population, 1980-90
					Bottom 20%	Top 20%	
United States	$21,790	0.9%	<5%	76 years	4.7%	41.9%	1.1%
Canada	20,470	1.0	<5	77	5.7	40.2	1.1
OECD Average	20,170	0.6	4	77	—	—	0.8
Japan	25,430	0.6	<5	79	8.7	37.5	0.7
Mexico	2,490	2.0	13	70	n.a.	n.a.	2.9
Chile	1,940	1.7	7	72	n.a.	n.a.	2.3
Argentina	2,370	1.3	5	71	n.a.	n.a.	1.8
Venezuela	2,560	2.7	12	70	4.7	50.6	2.8
Korea	5,400	1.1	<5	71	n.a.	n.a.	3.5
Singapore	11,160	2.2	<5	74	5.1	48.9	2.2
China	370	1.4	27	70	n.a.	n.a.	n.a.

Source: World Bank.

and other benefits in the high-wage area? Will it push up the wage rates and benefits in the low-wage area? Will it promote equitable and efficient growth, or will it stunt development in various parts of the bloc? These questions are hardly academic, because many economic, social, and political variables depend on their answers.

A major question is whether there will be upward or downward convergence of compensation rates, unit labor costs, and benefit levels. As one author in this volume, Clark Reynolds of Stanford University, puts it, upward convergence happens when the levels in the lower nation come up to the levels in the higher nation. Downward convergence happens when the levels in the higher nation come down to the levels in the lower nation. These two possibilities, of course, entail quite different political and developmental results.

Mainstream economic theory argues that the greatest gains in efficiency and growth tend to come from linking those regions that have very different labor, productivity levels, and capital market and natural resource conditions. If two nations are similar in detail, then they will probably have similar comparative advantages. Thus, by linking them in a regional trading bloc, the possibilities for increased economic efficiency and growth may be small. However, if two nations have major differences in their labor, product, and capital and natural resource markets, then they will probably also have great differences in their comparative advantages. When these two nations are linked in a trading bloc, then the possibilities for economic efficiency and increased growth tend to be very large, according to mainstream economic theory.[2]

DIFFERENT APPROACHES

The possibility of large gains from economic integration also creates the possibility of large labor market and social displacement. The formation of a regional trading bloc will often create winners and losers. The three major blocs are developing very different approaches toward handling labor market and social displacement. The European Community is forming a written social charter, while the NAFTA is not. However, President Clinton has said that he will push for side agreements that deal with labor and environmental issues. The bloc that is forming in East Asia is purely economic, and it is not held together by any treaty.

There is a growing debate concerning how much the NAFTA should become involved in social charter issues. Or, as two analysts recently put it:

> In broad terms, this issue boils down to a question that is becoming familiar in all international trade forums: How far, and by what means, is it legitimate for one country to use trade policies to respond to the domestic policies of its trading partners? There is nothing remarkable, for example, about a country changing its tariffs in response to changes in another country's tariffs. But what about a country changing its tariffs in response to another country's labor standards, environmental controls, or social welfare programs?...It is possible to argue for a minimal free trade position that makes the smallest possible demands on domestic policies. At the other extreme is a maximal position that submits a wide range of domestic policies to the control of an international agency.[3]

Some analysts have viewed the formation of the North American regional trading bloc as a "win-win" proposition for both the high and low wage regions. They predict that wages, employment levels, and productivity will all increase in the United States, Canada, and Mexico due to the NAFTA. These results will be created by a more efficient allocation of resources and increased regional specialization.

Other analysts see the formation of a regional trading bloc in North America as a "lose-lose" proposition. They predict that not only will wages, employment levels, and productivity be diminished in the United States due to the NAFTA, but also that Mexico will be hurt in the process. They predict that several important Mexican industries—such as agriculture and various parts of the manufacturing sector—will be hurt by competition from the north.

Most of the authors in this volume do not place themselves in a "win-win" or "lose-lose" camp. Instead, most view the formation of a North American trading bloc as a process that will generate significant winners and losers. The winners may outnumber the losers; nevertheless, the displacement could be significant in the transition process.

Many of the authors point to ways that the "losers" in the integration process can be helped. They also point to ways that the development process can be beneficial to both the high-wage and the low-wage areas. In the long run, the NAFTA model of development will be able to continue to function only if it addresses the benefits as well as the costs associated with the integration process.

FUNDAMENTAL CONCERNS

A fundamental concern of many of the authors in this volume is the implications of the NAFTA for wages and investment patterns. In an effort to predict the NAFTA's winners and losers, Clark Reynolds, in Chapter 2, attempts to link macroeconomic and microeconomic theory, and he questions whether these economies will converge. Reynolds defines two types of convergence—upward and downward—and highlights the three stages in convergence between productivity and wages. To evaluate the convergence climate of the 1990s, Reynolds discusses the problems of convergence in an open economy with very different wage levels.

Results from Reynolds' NAFTA model show sustained growth potential for Mexico via consumption spending. The model also indicates that the winners from integration are low-skilled labor in Mexico and high-skilled labor and capital in the United States. The losers are high-skilled labor in Mexico and low-skilled labor in the United States. Reynolds places a question mark beside the status of capital in Mexico.

Harley Shaiken, in Chapter 3, notes that if the promise of freer trade is to be realized, then paying attention to the implications of the NAFTA's social charter should be the foundation of further economic integration in this hemisphere. To develop this argument, he addresses three issues. First, he examines Mexico's potential in terms of manufacturing and high-tech production. The author contends that a macroeconomic overview of productivity data does not reveal the substantial modernization of manufacturing plants for products like autos and computers. However, in a growing number of Mexican plants, quality and productivity rival the best in Japan and the United States. Second, the author discusses the relationship between rising productivity and wages in Mexico. The historic link between rising productivity and wages that allows workers to enter the middle class has largely been absent in Mexico. Shaiken warns that a situation in which Mexico achieves First World productivity at Third World wages could exert a downward pressure on wages throughout North America.

Third, Shaiken examines the likely impacts on labor markets in the United States of an economic integration process that fails to address critical social issues. He examines the influence of integration on collective bargaining and wage setting. A relatively small movement of high-wage manufacturing jobs to Mexico could exert a significant demonstration effect for both collective bargaining and the nonunion sector. The fundamental choice for the United States is either pursuing a high-wage, high-skill strategy or slipping into competition based on low wages and diminished skills. In the context of Mexico's emerging potential as a high-tech export platform coupled with sluggish U.S. wage increases, Shaiken states that the structure of Mexican labor markets could have unprecedented influence on labor markets in the U.S. and Canada.

In discussing the investment issue, Isaac Cohen, in Chapter 4, asserts that the benefits of the NAFTA will be realized if trade liberalization generates increased levels of investment. In attempting to assess the agreement's impact, the author suggests that it is necessary to focus on other dynamic effects such as factor price equalization. Equalization is an inevitable consequence of free trade between two countries, and the resulting increase or decrease in wages may cause economic and social dislocations. Cohen states that in an agreement like the NAFTA, however, gains for labor are ensured even though the economic integration is taking place between a developed and a developing country.

The relationship between the U.S. and Puerto Rico is used as an example of successful trade liberalization between a less developed country and a developed nation. Although Cohen acknowledges the Puerto Rican experience cannot simply be repeated elsewhere, he believes that there are equalization and adjustment lessons to be learned from the island's success in the pharmaceutical industry.

In addition, Cohen stresses the need for socially equitable adjustments. Devaluing currencies, for example, makes Latin American wages attractive to foreign investors, but at the cost of impoverishing workers. Competitiveness based on social equity, he says, requires better training for the labor force, leading to better salaries and improved income distribution.

Richard Rothstein, in Chapter 5, proposes that it is impossible to integrate a high-wage, high-skill economy with a low-wage, low-skill economy while hoping to maintain the former at its high-wage status. In fact, he states that the Fair Labor Standards Act was adopted under similar conditions—to prevent the deterioration of the Northeast after the flight of manufacturing to low-wage regions in the South. The author is concerned with the problems of integrating Mexican wages with the U.S. economy, the drastic decline of Mexican wages as a result of policy intervention, and the issue of labor standards. In a parallel with the Great Depression, Rothstein highlights the plight of Mexican workers who are unable to consume the products they produce, concluding that in such a climate, U.S. export markets in Mexico will not grow.

Van R. Whiting, Jr., in Chapter 6, maintains that the movement toward free trade in the NAFTA and the Americas can be explained in three ways. First, liberalization and economic integration respond to underlying flows of goods, people, capital, and information. North American free trade is supported by functional interdependence. The NAFTA is built on a base of low transaction costs and high levels of information flows, opportunities for industrial restructuring, and strong political leadership.

Second, new patterns of foreign investment, linked to the increased competition within industries in the major developed markets of Europe, Asia, and North America, produced a new set of opportunities for nontraditional exports from developing countries. Beyond the efficiencies of specialization, global restructuring of industry and particularly the possibilities for new investments in regional markets help create a new interest in economic liberalism in developing countries.

Third, the failure of statism and of inward-oriented development in the 1980s created the basis for new political coalitions to emerge, reflected in an emerging consensus in the Americas. The main challenge is building a political coalition able to provide stable policy. In an era of uncertainty, predictability is more important than speed; stable and predictable policies are crucial. The primary challenge is designing policies that will be sustainable in the face of inevitable opposition from those previously privileged sectors that retain political power and resist the imposition of specific losses, even if they are offset by generalized gains.

HEMISPHERIC INTEGRATION AND DEVELOPMENT

To better understand the NAFTA model of development, Joseph Grunwald, in Chapter 7, provides a review of Latin America's economic heritage, its relationship with the United States, and issues involved in hemispheric integration. He notes that recent integration efforts may be more efficient because Latin American countries have unilaterally reduced trade barriers. For the same reason, fear of trade agreements with the North has subsided and many countries in the region are actively seeking free trade arrangements with the United States. Mexico is a unique case because the NAFTA recognizes the already existing intimate economic relationship with the United States. The fact that other countries seek a free trade agreement with the North in the face of a postwar decline in the importance of the United States in their total trade confirms the belief that their primary objective, even more so than for Mexico, is not trade expansion but the bolstering of domestic and foreign confidence in their economies.

Sidney Weintraub, in Chapter 8, considers the macroeconomic implications of the NAFTA for Mexico in the context of how the country has managed its economy during the restructuring process that began in the 1980s. He asserts that the symbolic insurance provided by the NAFTA has increased investment because of anticipation of free trade and certainty of treatment. Although static and dynamic studies predict economic growth as a result of free trade, Weintraub cautions that all of the conclusions are based on the assumption of well managed domestic policy.

The NAFTA can serve as a model for future North-South agreements, but it is unclear how closely the model will be followed. The author believes that the possibility for economic integration based on the NAFTA model depends on the state of the industrial structure in the developing country. If the developing country is an exporter of raw materials, for instance, North-South integration will be relatively meaningless. In fact, it is Weintraub's hope that more subregional integration occurs among member developing countries. Regarding nonmembers, the author suggests that the NAFTA sign agreements with subregional groups rather than permit the accession of numerous single nations. For the United States, the short-term effect of the NAFTA on the macroeconomy may be hardly noticeable. But in the long term, according to Weintraub, Mexican growth translates into growth for U.S. exports because Mexico's marginal propensity to import is higher than that of the United States.

Rudolf M. Buitelaar, in Chapter 9, focuses on the structure and dynamics of production and trade, making a distinction between the relationships among Latin American countries and between Latin America and the outside world. He questions whether a development strategy that pursues intra-regional integration between developing countries is different from a global export-led development strategy. Buitelaar hypothesizes that it is part of the same strategy—integration between Latin American countries is one part of a global opening-up strategy that pursues general export-led growth. Second, he wonders if there are differences between the composition of trade flows among Latin American countries and the composition of trade flows between Latin American countries and the rest of the world.

Buitelaar argues that regional markets offer opportunities to develop industrial exports that are likely to have important technological learning effects. A case can be made that regional integration should be promoted by explicit policy measures, complementary to extra-regional trade, not opposed to it, because openness of markets to third parties goes hand in hand with increased intra-regional export efforts.

MEXICAN VIEWPOINTS

Of the three NAFTA partners, the effects of the NAFTA will be most obvious in Mexico. Not surprisingly, there is a diverse set of opinions in Mexico about the NAFTA's consequences. Adolfo Aguilar Zinser, in Chapter 10, begins by addressing several issues regarding the NAFTA that he believes remain unchallenged in Mexico. For instance, the author says that there is general agreement that Mexico must sign a regional trade agreement with the U.S. to build and establish conditions for future development, but the options available are no longer as contradictory or exclusive as those presented in the past. The issues that are debated, however, include ways to increase U.S. investment and production in Mexico, deregulation, and the role of the state in the economy. Aguilar then discusses the sequence of events that are expected to ultimately reduce the flow of migration from Mexico to the U.S. and the concern over the disparity between the Mexican and American economies. Criticism of free trade is based on what Aguilar labels the "10 terms of redefinition." He concludes that Mexico deserves a state-of-the-art trade agreement, like Europe's Maastricht Treaty, that includes a social charter, standardization of norms, or compensatory investments.

To accumulate capital for further economic growth and to create the adjustment mechanisms necessary for the transition from a closed system to an open one, Gustavo del Castillo V., in Chapter 11, writes that Mexican policymakers must look to transitional economics that focus on the short to medium term while laying the groundwork for long-range policies. Some of the macroeconomic conditions governing Mexican liberalization include redefining the state as a social actor; application of self-imposed and exogenously imposed limits on the intervention of the state in the economy; and crafting necessary economic and social conditions for putting this redefinition into practice. The new role envisioned for foreign investment has already attracted new commitments from transnationals such as Nissan and Ford. However, the author cautions that the NAFTA shifts anticipation of economic growth to Mexico's external sector while allowing the internal market to remain constricted through wage and fiscal policies.

According to a 1989-91 survey, small and medium-sized manufacturing firms in Mexico were enthusiastic about free trade. However, many said they must entirely restructure their organizations and would need financial, computational, and communication services to compete. Because these firms believe that competitiveness lies in increased technological know-how and are seeking access to human and capital resources, del Castillo states that Mexico must have an industrial policy that emphasizes educational and technical achievement, coupled with a monetary policy that frees and accounts for the capital needs of these industries.

Daniel Szabo, in Chapter 12, examines the NAFTA in the context of both old and new developing models adopted by Latin America in the past few years—models that have not solved the competing goals of growth and equality. Szabo acknowledges that the NAFTA alone will not solve Mexico's development problems, but he believes that the potential rewards will outweigh the costs. Although it provides for a Trade Commission and Secretariat, the agreement will not create common development financial institutions, coordinated economic and social policies, or powerful supra-national governing bodies. Given this scenario, Szabo says it is unlikely, though not impossible, that a social development fund or common financial institution will be created. However, he believes that Mexico is the principal beneficiary of the NAFTA, with Canada gaining largely by avoiding discrimination in a Mexican market. Because the economies of the U.S. and Canada are much larger than Mexico's, Szabo states that the overall impact of the NAFTA will probably not be as significant as critics and supporters believe. He concludes by emphasizing the important symbolic and political role of the NAFTA for Latin American governments who view the agreement as the "new" U.S. policy toward the region. From this perspective, Szabo concludes that the development of the NAFTA's social dimension becomes even more important.

To discuss the question of international labor migration from Mexico to the United States, Jorge Bustamante, in Chapter 13, begins by examining some basic assumptions. First, the NAFTA was a political strategy presented as the best option for economic development in Mexico. Second, Mexico willingly entered the negotiations with the United States, not as a result of the asymmetry of power between the two countries. In fact, in an unprecedented move, the Mexican government opened the process of consultation to representatives of different sectors of the economy—such as business, labor, and academia—and organized an advisory committee on agreement negotiations. Finally, the two sides of the border possess significant differences in the definition of the question of labor migration. The United States defines the problem as a crime-related phenomenon, while Mexico considers it an economic and labor-related problem.

Although calculating illegal immigration is difficult, Bustamante notes the results of a study conducted in Tijuana since 1987. The study estimates that no significant impact will be felt in the phenomenon of undocumented immigration in the first 5 years after the signing of the NAFTA. In 6 to 10 years, the impact will be no more than a 25 percent reduction, while the study predicts a maximum reduction of 50 percent in 11 to 15 years.

CANADIAN VIEWPOINTS

Canada's interests in the NAFTA may be the least understood of the three partners. Ronald Wonnacott, in Chapter 14, explores the high points and pitfalls of the NAFTA from a Canadian perspective. Through participation in the NAFTA, Wonnacott believes that Canada has avoided discrimination it would otherwise have faced in Mexico in competing with duty-free U.S. goods. In other words, the Canadian government has been successful in gaining access to a rapidly growing Mexican market on terms as favorable as those of the United States. Another benefit is Canadian tariff-free access to inexpensive supplies of intermediate goods produced in Mexico. Wonnacott believes that, in one important way, the NAFTA is superior to treaties like the GATT, which allows developing countries to maintain many of their own barriers to liberalized imports. The NAFTA has effectively told Mexico and other future participants that if they want to participate in the agreement, they must be prepared to remove their own trade barriers.

Wonnacott believes that the NAFTA is an improvement over the CUSFTA for Canada in a number of ways: for example, it modifies and extends duty drawbacks and provides greater discipline over standards. More important, all three countries will have the same low or zero MFN tariff on computer imports from non-NAFTA countries, thus making rules of origin unnecessary. This sets a precedent in future negotiations for the elimination of the problems rules of origin create in a world in which firms are having increasing difficulty in tracing what has been produced where.

Ann Weston, in Chapter 15, suggests that for many Canadians, evaluation of the NAFTA must be seen through the lens of experience under the CUSFTA. Although the CUSFTA coincided with macroeconomic problems and global recession, Weston suggests that lessons learned from the agreement include the need for adjustment assistance and improved monitoring and evaluation of labor and environmental standards in all three countries. She says the issue of enforcement of both adjustment measures and labor standards has been raised in Canada, with some proponents favoring a social charter similar to the European Community's. If the NAFTA fails to deal directly with the adjustment issues likely to arise in Mexico, it must provide special rules sensitive to the country's different level of development and liberalization. Also, the phasing and extent of liberalization in particular sectors must allow for asymmetric or relative reciprocity. For example, Mexico can address this need through a longer phase-in period for meeting the common rules.

BUSINESS AND LABOR VIEWPOINTS

The business and labor communities are focused on the NAFTA, for the consequences of the agreement will have the greatest impact on their interests. John D. Tessier, in Chapter 16, asserts that the public sector must undergo the same restructuring process experienced by industries and corporations wanting to remain competitive internationally. Because this restructuring is occurring on a global basis, Tessier states that the choice for Latin American policymakers is no longer what direction to take, but how quickly to make the transition to market economies. Moving from a protected to an open market environment not only causes massive changes in government responsibilities and procedures, but also realigns the role of the business community within this new economic structure. To illustrate this point, Tessier briefly discusses IBM's role in Latin America and shares knowledge gained from the corporation's own restructuring process. For instance, trade blocs have forced IBM to organize its business around trading areas to avoid prohibitive investment costs. However, such a structure also allows IBM to provide more support for the members of the region without duplicating every management service in each country.

William C. Doherty, in Chapter 17, predicts that the NAFTA would result in a major job loss for the U.S. and that it would push down U.S. wage rates. Although the NAFTA has generated some conflict between the United States and Canada over this issue, he asserts that the greatest conflict has been between American and Mexican interests. According to Doherty, corporations export jobs to Mexico for one economic advantage—low wages. With millions of Mexican workers unable to find jobs in the Maquiladoras, illegal immigration into the United States has increased. The labor movement is also concerned about working conditions and the enforcement of environmental regulations in this area. To address these concerns, the American labor movement is conducting a series of meetings with their Mexican counterparts because the AFL-CIO is not satisfied with the NAFTA as it now stands.

Although the AFL-CIO has concluded that a trade agreement with Mexico is not inherently bad if it were a fair trade agreement, Doherty stresses that the U.S. relationship with Mexico should have the same degree of dignity as that of the European Community's relationship with the poorer nations of that continent. Just as the EC has developed a substantial development plan to raise the economic status of those countries, Doherty believes a similar plan would have to equalize disparities between the three countries without taking jobs away from Americans. The American labor movement would like the NAFTA to guarantee some provisions designed to protect the workers of all three nations—decent Social Security benefits, strict enforcement of labor laws, and rights to freedom of association and collective bargaining—all enforced by trade sanctions.

Eugene W. Zeltmann, in Chapter 18, discusses the structure and role of the sector advisory committees in the NAFTA negotiations. The Industry Sector Advisory Committee for Capital Goods (ISAC-2), one of 17 committees, works to remove barriers to the free conduct of trade in capital goods, including the area of heavy electrical equipment. The Committee was asked to evaluate the trade agreement, and it presented to Congress a list of the NAFTA's pluses and minuses. Zeltmann says the Committee told Congress that the NAFTA would go a long way in eradicating many trade barriers and "unshackle the creative energies of the people of the three North American signatories."

In its evaluation, ISAC-2 concluded that the NAFTA's net impact on U.S. employment would be positive. However, the Committee recommended assistance and job training for workers who lose jobs and are unable to find employment with their current skills. On environmental issues, the Committee views the NAFTA as a "green agreement" that will result in substantial environmental improvement when implemented. To illustrate this point, Zeltmann highlights the increased efficiency of today's combined-cycle power-generation plants that utilize natural gas for the production of energy.

Juan de Nigris, in Chapter 19, examines the effects of trade liberalization on Mexican economic and social policy. He stresses that not all of Mexico's problems can be solved through the NAFTA, but involvement in the agreement is an important piece of the country's economic integration strategy. Furthermore, the success of the agreement will not be the result of "good" or "bad" negotiating, but will depend on its ability to develop clear rules that define behavior in regional economies. The rules are also important because de Nigris believes that they may inspire confidence for investors in the Mexican, Canadian, and American economies. Under the NAFTA, the United States should benefit from Mexico's high propensity to import U.S. goods, especially critical capital and high-tech products. De Nigris also points out the United States will gain in the intellectual property and service exports sectors, as Mexico seeks assistance in areas such as transportation and telecommunications.

According to de Nigris, the history of his company, VITRO, serves as proof that Mexico has been fighting to achieve and maintain international competitiveness and economic efficiency for a long time. Mexican companies are reacting to global realities as much as regional ones. They are working quickly to take advantage of economic opportunities that began well before the NAFTA. In their push for economic integration, these companies have not forgotten their social responsibility and many, like VITRO, have numerous social programs for their workers. Although VITRO is just one example, de Nigris believes that many companies have followed the same developmental path, with others ready to continue the processes of modernization.

A SOCIAL CHARTER?

Our final authors examine the European social charter as a possible model for the NAFTA and the extent to which nongovernmental organizations have become players in the NAFTA debate. Reiner Hoffmann, in Chapter 20, maintains that although the success of labor market policies in Europe can be compared to the NAFTA market of the future only to a limited degree, he believes that the EC experience shows the agreement must progress beyond the status of pure market integration if it is to be successful. In contrast to the neoliberal approach of the NAFTA, for instance, European integration has always been accompanied by the attempt to take the social dimension of the single market into consideration. In his chapter, Hoffmann addresses three central aspects of Europe's social dimension that he believes can supply important insights to successful implementation of the NAFTA—the European dialogue, the European Social Fund, and the European Regional Fund.

Cathryn L. Thorup, in Chapter 21, insists that in today's world, international relations bear scant resemblance to earlier models based upon the interaction of unitary rational actors.

Nongovernmental organizations (NGOs) working in concert with counterpart groups around the world are contributing to a transnationalization of civil society. Thorup asserts that the significance of "citizen diplomacy" for North America first became apparent during the NAFTA negotiations in 1990. Subsequent cross-border organizing and coalition-building have influenced the shape and substance of an integrated North America, making it clear that relations between the United States, Canada, and Mexico are no longer the exclusive domain of economic and political elites. As nations find themselves unable to manage their relations on a strict government-to-government basis, the process of negotiating economic integration has become more complex, forcing negotiators to take more issues and actors into account. At the same time, Thorup points out that NGOs are weaving together the interests of citizens from each country, contributing to the formation of an evolving sense of societal interdependence. This trend affects decisionmaking not only in the commercial arena, but in other issues such as immigration.

UNCHARTED WATERS

The North American Free Trade Agreement is an experiment in largely uncharted territory. Never before has there been such a discrepancy in levels of economic development between the partners to such an agreement. The NAFTA has aroused interest across industrial and governmental sectors and around the globe, for if it is ratified in the United States, it will be a laboratory for those concerned about what such agreements will do to wages, to labor mobility, to labor unions, to investment, to living standards, and to economic development. Whether one supports or opposes the NAFTA, it must be examined carefully. If the agreement benefits only a small group and injures many, then the NAFTA will have failed. However, if it is successful—by which we mean if increased trade is facilitated, investment is raised, job loss is very minimal, job creation is substantial, wages are brought up, and free trade unions are expanded—then the NAFTA will be the precursor for more regional free trade agreements and greater mutual understanding. It will be a positive example to other nations. This is our hope, and we will be watching carefully.

Notes

1. For more on regional trading blocs, see Richard S. Belous and Rebecca S. Hartley, *The Growth of Regional Trading Blocs in the Global Economy* (Washington, D.C.: National Planning Association, 1990).

2. Paul R. Krugman and Maurice Obstefeld, *International Economics: Trade and Policy* (New York: HarperCollins, 1991), pp. 24-27, 110, 114.

3. Jonathan Lemco and William B.P. Robson, "A Social Charter for North America?," in *Ties Beyond Trade: Labor and Environmental Issues Under the NAFTA*, ed. Jonathan Lemco and William B.P. Robson (Toronto, Ont.: Canadian-American Committee [National Planning Association], 1993), pp. 4-5.

PART II

IMPLICATIONS OF THE NAFTA FOR WAGES AND INVESTMENT

2. The NAFTA and Wage Convergence: A Case of Winners and Losers

by Clark W. Reynolds

The NAFTA will generate winners and losers, and economic theory can help us predict who will be in each group. However, it is interesting to note that there is not a single textbook that effectively puts macro- and microeconomics together; this fact is simply a commentary on the social sciences and not on the pressing problems of social reality.

UPWARD OR DOWNWARD CONVERGENCE

To understand the economic impacts of the NAFTA, we have to relate output to productivity, productivity to wages, and wages to employment and income for three economies with dissimilar levels of productivity and different economic and social structures. We also have to make our estimates in a dynamic context and in such a way that the three nations can coalesce and feed back on output again, presumably through consumption and investment. Finally, this analysis must be conducted in an internationally integrating framework. Although that is certainly not the kind of problem that you would want to find on your Econ 101 exam, this is the macro- and microeconomic dilemma that we are supposed to address. To answer the question regarding the link between macro and micro, we are basically asking: do these economies converge?

First, we have to define convergence. Convergence can be seen as one of two possible scenarios: upward convergence and downward convergence of productivity, factor prices, and wages in the North American economies. Upward convergence means that those starting at the low end move up toward those at the high end in such a way that the ones at the high end do not go down. That is not an easy thing to accomplish. Upward convergence is a good political scenario for all participants.

Downward convergence happens when productivity, factor prices, and wages increase at the low end while decreasing at the high end. This convergence is more common. It is also a politically volatile situation, especially for Canada and the United States. The other possibility is divergence where there is a widening of the gap between the high-wage and the low-wage regions. In recent years there has been convergence among the advanced industrial countries. Essentially we have seen countries of the Organization for Economic Cooperation and Development (OECD) engaged in a certain amount of convergence, and for the most part it has been upward convergence. In Japan, upward convergence has been astronomical. Even Germany, which has fallen in terms of its OECD ranking, has not suffered a decline in real wages. There is also evidence of a definite average tendency toward convergence in Europe in the 1970s and 1980s. Convergence in Europe is associated with economic integration of the European Community (EC) and the European Free Trade Agreement (EFTA). Trade investment and migration have both played an important role, especially for the poorer southern European economies. In the United States, there is a large body of literature among American economic historians showing convergence between the North and South after World War II.

Despite some convergence in productivity in the late 1970s, nonconvergence between Mexico and the rest of North America is very clear in our statistics. Clearly, the 1980s was a decade of divergence in productivity and real wages in the North American case. In the European case, there has been some divergence between northern and southern Italy, northern and southern Spain, and other regions of the European continent.

STAGES OF CONVERGENCE

There are three stages in convergence between productivity and wages. The first stage is a convergence attempt in productivity. The simplest measure is to estimate output value added per worker. Value added per worker is something that is not converging between the United States and Mexico. The next stage is factor price convergence. Factor price convergence means that if trade takes place in goods and services between two economies, then labor compensation (i.e., factor prices) may converge. No factor price equalization theorem discusses simple wage convergence until labor has the same character (e.g., capital level) in the two economies. The third stage is wage convergence. Between standard labor unit convergence and wage convergence, we have to convert labor in the low country into standard wage labor units comparable to the high country. To accomplish this, we must add capital, technology and human capital to the low-wage labor. Thus, you can have factor price convergence between the United States and Mexico and not wage convergence. Wage convergence is the last thing likely to occur.

The labor market plays a very important role in this convergence process. If you integrate, then microeconomics indicates that whatever the wage level, workers will be employed until the so-called marginal value product (i.e., benefits the worker produces) equals the wage (i.e., cost of the worker). But one does not change the wage. In the macro model, you have two options. If you are cagey, you say "I can't do anything about the wage, that is the way it is." In this situation, you then alter aggregate demand and output, and employment changes. But in many macroeconomic models, the wage is determined interdependently with the supply and demand of labor—an elastic supply of labor creates lower real wages than a scarce supply of labor in a closed economy

AN OPEN ECONOMY

What will happen if you have an open economy? That is our problem, especially since we have one wage in Mexico and a very different wage in the United States. There is one really sneaky way around this problem called the factor price equalization theorem. The theorem says that under several strong assumptions, (e.g., labor is the same quality in both countries, there is similar technology in both countries, and there are no increasing returns to scale), trade between the two parties will result in equal factor prices. The problem with that is these conditions apply only somewhat between Canada and the United States. Between Mexico and the United States, we do not have a factor price equalization area. Such an area requires the same kind of labor in both countries, the same kind of capital, and no complete specialization—conditions that simply do not exist in reality. If one country has lots of labor and the other has lots of capital, you are going to move into specialized points, preventing the formation of a factor price equalization area.

How do you get factor price equalization in the above situation? All you have to do is move capital south to add to labor, and labor north to add to capital. When you do enough of that, a factor price equalization area is created. But the NAFTA only allows capital movement between countries, and capital movement without labor movement distorts the picture. I am not against capital moving; I am simply saying that you cannot solve the problem of wage trends unless so much capital moves south that it becomes impossible for the United States to have the same historic wage levels. Thus, if we are going to have factor price equalization between the United States and Mexico, only letting capital move south will not produce this result. U.S. wages are going to decrease unless we allow Mexican labor to move north as capital from the United States moves south. This may not be politically correct or viable, but there is no way around this problem.

The other condition is that technology as well as managerial skills must move south. When combining capital and labor to integrate this market, it is necessary to have the same ratios for the pool of managerial skills, technology, and capital in Mexico to create an arrangement comparable to the most labor-intensive parts of the United States. I think such a scenario is possible, but that it is a very difficult thing to accomplish under the present set of laws, institutions, and regulations. Within such a framework, you are not going to have factor price equalization and, of course, you are not going to have wage equalization.

What happens in the above process will favor owners of capital because they will earn market penetration rents (i.e., returns above normal profits). There will be excess profits, or rents, that will go to capital and make these markets adjust. Also, there will be excess rents going to labor that is able to get over the various thresholds and enter the U.S. labor market. Thus, labor can make the rents by moving north, and capital can make the rents by moving south. Also, capital in the south can make the rents by combining with labor in the south.

What about labor in the north? There can only be upward convergence if the north grows fast enough to reduce unemployment and absorb labor force growth. This requires a fundamental transformation of the savings and investment behavior of the north. I believe that capital will inevitably move south, and that means that if the United States is going to "run faster to stay in the same place" or move ahead in terms of productivity, it must massively increase its savings and investment.

Thus, in the NAFTA model, profits are going to take most of these rents in the short and medium run. Through collective bargaining, workers may push for a share of these rents. Also, there are significant gains to be had from the diffusion of consumption in Mexico, as its productivity goes up, and as the returns to its population diffuse. There will be sustained growth potential in Mexico, but it will not come from trade. While trade will discipline the Mexican market and encourage Mexican industries to behave more competitively, the return from diffusion of the gains in growth via consumption spending are going to be very important for Mexico.

LOW- AND HIGH-SKILLED LABOR

Finally, there is the social dimension. We have built a binational computable general equilibrium model for the two countries, which divided up the labor force into low- and high-skilled labor and capital. The model definitely shows that the winners from integration are low-skilled labor in Mexico, and high-skilled labor and capital in the United States. The losers are low-skilled labor in the United States, and there is a question mark about capital in Mexico. These results indicate that there are cross-border constituencies between yuppies and capitalists in the United States and workers in Mexico. On the other side, low-skilled labor in the United States and capitalists in Mexico are in the same boat. One painful side effect for yuppies and capitalists in Mexico is the higher prices they will have to pay for services and labor-intensive goods relative to what they are paying now. This will be caused by a scarce labor situation and is going to affect their whole lifestyle.

I believe that we are going to have to create a binational or trinational social pact with cross-border constituencies. Only Europe has tried to do this, and it has taken the EC many years to have a social program fully in place.

Suppose we were to bring about factor price convergence in North America, including Mexico, and that eventually led to wage convergence. Even in that case, we face a dilemma. We have to consider low wages in other parts of the world. How do we have this diffuse itself internationally, and how can we get a social pact that goes beyond North America or the EC? This is a problem that probably will be worrying us for the rest of our productive lives.

3. *The NAFTA, a Social Charter, and Economic Growth*

by Harley Shaiken

Many observers have commented that expanded trade in North America offers the promise for further development in Mexico and for economic growth in the United States and Canada. A word of caution, however, is in order: increased trade offers the promise, not the certainty, of these new benefits. Several scenarios of enhancing trade could lead in a much different direction, eroding wages in the United States and Canada, stunting wage growth in Mexico, and diminishing worker rights throughout the continent.

The context of the proposed trade agreement is important to understand its potential impact on labor and labor markets. The NAFTA does not represent a disjunction from what has occurred in the past, particularly in the 1980s, but rather an expansion and an acceleration of existing trends. In the area of investment rights and guarantees, the agreement is the culmination of over a decade of significant economic liberalization in Mexico. No such harmonization process, however, has taken place in the labor area, leaving labor rights and their enforcement far apart in the three economies.

A SOCIAL CHARTER

To fulfill the promise of expanded trade, I argue that a vital step is to move toward common labor standards—emphasizing basic worker and union rights—in the context of a North American social charter. In fact, this charter ought to be the foundation of further economic integration in the Western Hemisphere. I plan to develop this argument by briefly addressing three questions. First, what is Mexico's potential in terms of manufacturing in general and high-tech production in particular? Second, what is the link between productivity growth and wages in Mexico, and what role does that link play? Third, what are the likely impacts on U.S. labor markets of increased integration in the absence of a social charter? Given the lack of harmonization in the labor area, we can gain an insight into what may happen in terms of future labor markets by examining the recent past.

Consider first Mexico's manufacturing capability. A macroeconomic overview of the Mexican economy does not accurately describe either Mexico's current position or the trajectory for its future. By simply examining productivity data, the popular perception is reinforced of Mexico as a low productivity, low technology manufacturing economy. By extension, the U.S. is a high-tech, high productivity economy, and a "natural," mutually beneficial fit exists between the two.

In fact, a new generation of Mexican manufacturing plants first went on line in the early 1980s with much different characteristics than the stereotypical low productivity, labor intensive facilities of previous years. These factories demonstrate a substantial degree of modernization in diverse sectors such as autos, consumer electronics, computers, and other manufacturing areas. These more advanced facilities also include plants in the in-bond or Maquiladora sector. "Second generation maquiladoras now incorporate much more advanced technology, more capital intensive methods," Wilson observes (1992, 4). If we scrutinize the track record of these more sophisticated plants over the past decade, we find that the quality and productivity of high-tech Mexican plants rival the best Japanese plants and often exceed U.S. standards. Therefore, trying to understand what future integration may look like requires examining both the history and the technological capabilities of these new plants. If we consider only the macroeconomic data, we merely gain a perspective on where the Mexican manufacturing base has been; by focusing on this new generation of cutting-edge facilities we are able to gain a sense of the direction in which Mexico is going.

What do these success cases look like on a micro level? They are hardly typical of Mexico's manufacturing base, but they do define the possibilities that exist for the future. For example, Ford's $500 million assembly and stamping plant in Hermosillo, Mexico, produced the second highest quality small car sold in North America in 1990. The quality of the Mexican-assembled Mercury Tracers was higher than the quality of Toyotas, Nissans, and other far better known subcompacts. In fact, the quality was considerably higher than a nearly identical model produced by Ford's Mazda affiliate in Japan, hardly an example of a low-tech or low-productivity manufacturing facility (Shaiken, 1990). Also, Nissan has manufactured its highest quality manual transaxle world-wide in Aguascalientes on a consistent basis (Shaiken, 1993).

Sony provides another example. The company assembles television sets in two nearby locations on both sides of the U.S-Mexican border; one plant is in Tijuana, the other is in Rancho Bernardo north of San Diego. Almost all the production of both plants is sold in the U.S. market and the quality of the two plants' products is so similar that their warranty numbers are not separated by Sony (Shaiken, 1993).

While these overall results are impressive, the technological underpinnings—the time frame and requirements necessary to set up production—are even more so. In particular, the speed with which manufacturing operations of this complexity can be set up on green field sites is remarkable. The Ford Hermosillo plant achieved quality preeminence in North America three years after going on line. A U.S. automaker's engine plant, producing an even more complex component in northern Mexico, achieved levels of quality and productivity comparable to this North American counterpart 18 months after it went into operation (Shaiken, 1987). Both plants hired young, inexperienced workers. The key to success in these and other plants was hiring employees whose basic education level was solid enough to facilitate intensive additional training. In fact, the education level was initially set at 12 years of schooling but was subsequently reduced to 9 years at the auto engine and assembly plants. (Nissan in Aguascalientes began with this lower level as its basic hiring criteria.)

While the infrastructure in these manufacturing areas is weak by U.S. standards, it has not presented an insurmountable obstacle to achieving worldclass productivity and quality. On the contrary, the aggregate trends in these and other industries reinforce the results found in these individual plants. Automobile engines, for example, are among the most complex manufactured components. In 1980, Mexico exported $30 million in auto engines, an amount that increased to $1.2 billion annually in 1992 (*Comercio Exterior*, 1993) and is predicted by the Mexican government to double to $2.4 billion annually by 1994 (Saavedra, 1993, 28).

EMPLOYMENT AND WAGES

Industrial expansions such as the one occurring in automobile engines indicate the scope of Mexico's industrial potential. It is clear that if Mexico manages its resources correctly, it could become a high-tech, export-oriented manufacturing base—a possibility that offers considerable promise for development. In terms of North American labor markets, however, Mexico's potential brings into contention not simply low-wage jobs (which many observers believe were already moving out of the country), but some of the highest wage North American manufacturing jobs as well. Here another central question arises: what factors determine the relationship between rising productivity and wages within Mexico? In an integrated continental economy where Mexican productivity and quality approach the best world standards, the linkage between productivity and wages in Mexico could prove influential in wage setting in the other two countries as well.

Real wages for manufacturing workers in Mexico fell through the floor in the 1980s, plummeting over 40 percent from their 1982 peak to their nadir in 1988 (BLS, 1993). While real wages have grown since 1991, the institutional forces that decoupled productivity increases from wage gains—controlled labor markets, government policies to encourage investment, and state-dominated unions, among other factors—are still in place.

In other words, the historic link between rising productivity and rising wages that has enabled workers in the United States and elsewhere to enter the middle class has largely been absent within the Mexican economy. The electronic equipment sector illustrates this point. Using the U.S. as a basis for comparison, overall productivity in Mexico went from 63 percent of U.S. levels in 1975 to 83 percent in 1984. During this period, wages dropped from 24 percent of U.S. levels to 15 percent (Blomstrom and Wolff, 1989, 25); see Figure 1. Moreover, if we examine the compensation of employees as a percent of gross domestic product (GDP), the share in Mexico peaked at 37.5 percent in 1981 and slid to 24.7 percent by 1990 (OECD, 1992, 255). Another measure, Mexican workers' earnings as a share of manufacturing value-added, plummeted from 44 percent in 1970 to 20 percent in the late 1980s, indicating increased polarization as well as declining real incomes (World Bank, 1992, 231).

Among many other factors, this drop in real income and relative shares of income reflects a highly controlled labor movement and few other alternatives (Middlebrook, 1991). As Laurence Whitehead states:

> The "official" labor movement has been at a loss to respond effectively to this new situation. Its appeals to state authorities go unacknowledged; its attempts to formulate alternative development strategies receive no response; its continuing loyalty to the regime earns no further rewards or influence; and the theoretical alternative of greater challenge and confrontation also offers no realistic prospect of greater bargaining power (1991, 82).

Echoing Whitehead's assessment, Castaneda and Heredia add that state policy effectively limits union leverage. ". . . the right to strike in Mexico is more a metaphor than anything else. Because of the union-exclusion clause and the unions' subordi-

FIGURE 1
Mexican Electronics Industry
Productivity and Compensation Compared to U.S. Levels, Selected Years, 1975-84

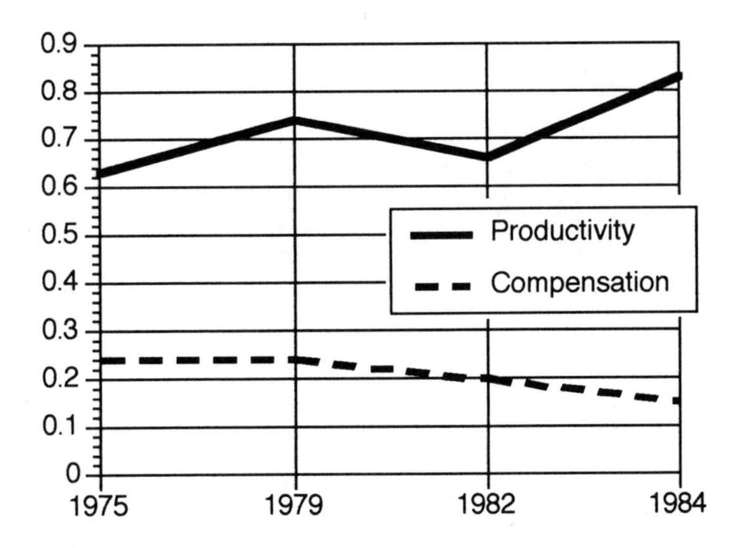

nation to the states and its party, the workers' ability to use the strike as a weapon is negligible" (1992, 681).

The controlled nature of the principal labor federation, Confederacion de Trabajadores de Mexico (CTM), is underscored if we look beyond the aggregate data and consider Mexican labor markets on a micro level. For example, wages are often higher in an older generation of far less productive automobile plants surrounding Mexico City than in a new generation of plants in the north with worldclass efficiency and quality. National or regional auto unions signed contracts that significantly lowered wages and benefits in the newer plants, often as part of government initiatives to attract investment (Middlebrook, 1991). This situation reflects both the relationship of the "official" labor movement and the states as well as the weakness of labor rights, which eliminates the possibility of realistic alternatives.

What are the implications of Mexico achieving First World productivity and quality and paying Third World wages? Not only could such an occurrence retard the growth of a consumer market in Mexico—workers capable of purchasing the products they produce—but it could also exert a downward pressure on wages throughout North America. The potential for Mexican economic and technological development is considerable and should be encouraged and applauded. But the impact that this development could have on labor markets in North America must be fully addressed in the current debate over the NAFTA.

LABOR MARKET IMPLICATIONS

This leads us to the third question: what are the likely impacts on U.S. labor markets of an economic integration process that fails to address these social issues? Real hourly wages have already slipped in the past decade in the U.S. In fact, real wages peaked at $9.50 an hour in 1978, slipping to about $8.00 an hour (or 1964 levels) by 1990. Moreover, unions exert a significantly diminished impact on wage setting within the U.S. economy, given the fact that the labor movement now represents less than 12 percent of the workforce.

Much of the attention to the labor implications of a NAFTA has focused on the question of net job gain or job loss. This is surely a central issue, and even the NAFTA proponents agree that there could be job dislocation within the U.S., despite their more optimistic predictions of net job gains. Rather than debate this point, I want instead to emphasize an area that may ultimately have an even greater impact—the influence of economic integration on collective bargaining and wage setting in the U.S. While much of the focus has been on how many jobs will be lost, relatively little has been asked about what will happen to the jobs that remain. Even a small movement of high-wage, high-skill manufacturing jobs to Mexico could exert a significant demonstration effect for both collective bargaining and the nonunion sector. *In other words, if you can make automobile engines with Japanese standards of quality and productivity at $4 or $5 an hour total compensation cost, why would you pay $40 an hour total compensation cost, which is roughly the current Big Three rate*? Under these circumstances, the harmonization that occurs between the U.S. and Mexican labor markets will likely be in a downwards direction.

THE HARD CHOICES

The fundamental choice then comes down to: Does the U.S. pursue a high-wage, high-skill strategy, or does it slip into competition based on low wages? The latter approach was voiced by Stanley Mihalek, Goodyear's Executive Vice President for

Manufacturing. He told the *New York Times* in the late 1980s that until real wage levels are reduced much closer to Brazilian and Korean levels, productivity gains cannot be passed along to wages and the U.S. remain competitive. But if Third World wages become the prerequisite for more competitive manufacturing, the U.S. could wind up with more competitive firms in a highly polarized and dislocated society.

To what extent could the possibility of relocating jobs to Mexico influence collective bargaining in the U.S.? In mid-1992, the *Wall Street Journal* published a poll of 455 leading corporate executives. About one-quarter of those interviewed stated that they were either very likely or at least somewhat likely to use the NAFTA as a bargaining tool to try to hold down wages in the U.S. If one-quarter of almost 500 executives admit this in such a politically sensitive poll, then the widespread use of economic integration as a bargaining chip in U.S. labor markets is certainly possible, if not likely. Furthermore, about 40 percent of those polled maintained that it is either very likely or somewhat likely that at least some of their firm's production will be moved to Mexico within the next several years. For companies with over $1 billion in annual sales, 55 percent of these executives indicated that some production could be transferred to Mexico.

In the context of Mexico's emerging potential as a high-tech export platform, the structure of Mexican labor markets could have unprecedented influence on labor markets in the United States and Canada. Moving toward a high-skill *and* high-wage strategy in all three countries requires the convergence of labor standards and labor rights in all three labor markets. Otherwise, labor standards, like water, could flow to the lowest point. Addressing this complex issue will require more than readjustment assistance, retraining programs, or funds that compensate those who are displaced in U.S. and Canadian labor markets, as important as these programs are. Instead, the integrated nature of the three labor markets raises a broader set of themes surrounding integrated development within North America. Among other issues, the subject of debt relief for Mexico must be put high on the agenda. Within the U.S. economy, broader labor law reform as a part of economic integration becomes a vital mechanism to ensure balance in the process of integration.

Finally, a central question concerns the efforts necessary to reestablish and ensure the relationship between productivity growth and wages within Mexico as part of an integrated North America. As Castaneda and Heredia put it, "Although it is difficult to legislate equal pay (though not guidelines for gradual equalization), it is possible to harmonize standards for collective bargaining, labor tribunals, the right to strike, and wider union freedom. With such power the workers themselves can achieve, over time, those levels of wages and benefits, as well as dignity in the workplace." (1992: 681).

With these issues at center stage, it is possible that expanded growth, trade, and economic integration can proceed in a way that benefits all three countries. But by simply focusing on investment guarantees, the severe downward pressure on labor markets in the U.S. and Canada will only continue while also increasing economic and social polarization within Mexico itself.

Bibliography

Anders, George. "Heading South: U.S. Companies Plan Major Moves Into Mexico." *Wall Street Journal* 24 Sept. 1992: R1.

Blomstrom, Magnus and Edward N. Wolff, "Multinational Corporations and Productivity Convergence in Mexico," National Bureau of Economic Research Working Paper No. 3141, cited in Blecker, Robert A. and William E. Spriggs, "Manufacturing Employment in North America: Where the Jobs Have Gone." *Economic Policy Institute Briefing Paper.* October 5, 1992.

Castaneda, Jorge and Carlos Heredia. "Another NAFTA: What a Good Agreement Should Offer." *World Policy Journal.* Fall/Winter 1992: 673-686.

Comercio Exterior. "Sumario estadistico," April 1993.

Middlebrook, Kevin J. "The Politics of Industrial Restructuring." *Comparative Politics* April 1991: 275-297.

Unions Workers, and the State in Mexico. La Jolla: Center for U.S.-Mexican Studies, University of California, San Diego, 1991.

Organization for Economic Cooperation and Development. *OECD Economic Surveys: Mexico 1991-1992.* New York: OECD, 1992.

Saavedra, Gustavo. "The Mexican Government's Perspective on NAFTA." Seventh Annual Conference of the Society of Automotive Analysts. Mexico City, May 11-14, 1993.

Shaiken, Harley and Stephen Herzenberg. *Automation and Global Production: Automobile Engine Production in Mexico, the United States, and Canada.* Monograph Series, No. 26. La Jolla, Center for U.S.-Mexican Studies, University of California, San Diego, 1987.

Shaiken, Harley. "Advanced Manufacturing and Mexico: The Auto and Electronics Sectors in U.S.-Mexico Trade and Investment." *Latin America Research Review* (forthcoming 1993).

———. *Mexico in the Global Economy: High Technology and Work Organization in Export Industries.* Monograph Series, No. 33. La Jolla, Center for U.S.-Mexican Studies, University of California, San Diego, 1990.

United States Department of Labor, Bureau of Labor Statistics, Office of Productivity and Technology. "Hourly compensation costs for production workers in manufacturing industries: Mexico, 1975-1992." Unpublished Data. March 1993.

———. "Real hourly compensation indexes, 1979-92, manufacturing production workers." Unpublished Data. March 1993.

United States Office of Technology Assessment. *U.S.-Mexico Trade: Pulling Together or Pulling Apart?* ITE-545. Washington, D.C.: U.S. Government Printing Office, October 1992.

Whitehead, Laurence. "Mexico's Economic Prospects: Implications for State-Labor Relations." *Unions, Workers, and the State in Mexico.* Ed. Kevin J. Middlebrook. La Jolla: Center for U.S.-Mexican Studies, University of California, San Diego, 1991.

Wilson, Patricia A. *Exports and Local Development: Mexico's New Maquiladoras.* Austin: University of Texas Press, 1992.

World Bank. *World Development Report 1992: Development and the Environment.* New York: Oxford University Press, 1992.

4. *The NAFTA's Winners and Losers: A Focus on Investment*

by Isaac Cohen

It is virtually an axiom that both winners and losers emerge from any change we experience. Is the situation any different with respect to the creation of the North American Free Trade Agreement? In addressing this issue, I will raise three points. First, in attempting to measure the NAFTA's impact on its winners and losers, we should focus on dynamic benefits, such as those derived from investment, rather than solely on static benefits. Second, after identifying the essential dynamic effects, we should discuss how to cxploit thcm whilc allowing for socially equitable adjustments. Third, we must address whether trade agreements should be open or closed.

There are now approximately 20 quantitative models in use in the NAFTA discussions. Each model attempts to measure the gains and losses that will be generated by the agreement. This cost-benefit area has more or less been covered, so I will focus on investment and the equalization of factor prices and standards. To simplify the investment issue, we will reap NAFTA's dynamic benefits if trade liberalization generates increased levels of investment.

FACTOR PRICE EQUALIZATION

One dynamic aspect is that trade liberalization should eventually create a healthier, more stable, and more inviting investment environment in Mexico.

Also, factor price equalization is one of the inevitable consequences of initiating truly free trade between two countries. However, the way factor prices are equalized can drastically alter the results. A dramatic increase or decrease in wages may cause both economic and social dislocation. In an agreement like the NAFTA, however, gains for labor are ensured. This is true even though the process of economic integration is taking place between a developed and a developing country.

In the developing country, for example, as investment increases, wages are likely to rise over time. Wages in the developed country, however, are not likely to decrease as much because of the role of labor unions. Although real wages in the U.S. have been declining, I firmly believe that the stickiness of wages due to the vigilance of labor unions will ensure that American workers do not suffer from factor price equalization.

A similar type of equalization is likely to occur with respect to environmental standards. I include environmental standards under factor prices because they influence the costs of factors of production. Although rules in the two countries should merge as a result of trade liberalization, the relative strength of concerned groups in the U.S., such as environmental groups, will prevent any corruption of U.S. environmental standards. As a result, Mexico will gradually be forced to raise its standards to the level of those in the U.S. In addition, in instances in which Mexican standards are already higher than those in the U.S., Mexico will be required to enforce them more rigorously.

These equalizations, along with increased investment, are some of the more important dynamic effects of NAFTA. In order to illustrate how this merging of standards might occur, I want to discuss Puerto Rico.

THE PUERTO RICAN EXPERIENCE

Puerto Rico is the only Spanish speaking part of the hemisphere that has enjoyed almost a century of free trade liberalization with the U.S. As such, the Puerto Rican economy is a laboratory in which we can analyze the results of a small, less developed economy integrating with a developed nation.

Among other effects of this integration, the Puerto Rican minimum wage is now equivalent to that in the U.S. Also, the small island has benefited greatly from trade in strategic sectors and is particularly strong in its pharmaceutical industry. In fact, 50 percent of all pharmaceutical products consumed in the U.S. come from Puerto Rico. On the other hand, agriculture, the mainstay of less developed economies, plays only a small role in Puerto Rico with less than 3 percent of gross national product (GNP).

Contrary to popular belief, Puerto Rico is probably one of the most industrialized regions of the world. Predictably, this creates problems with respect to environmental standards. Hyper-industrialization, however, has not prevented Puerto Rico from attempting to raise environmental standards to U.S. levels.

I agree that Puerto Rico's success in free trade cannot simply be repeated elsewhere. One advantage Puerto Rico has had is the free mobility of labor between itself and the U.S. It is, therefore, important to recognize that Puerto Rico is a singular case. We must also acknowledge that not every change in Puerto Rico resulting from free trade has been good. However, when critics argue that the NAFTA is unique because it brings together a developing country and a developed one for the first time, I have to insist that Puerto Rico was initially as underdeveloped, if not more so, than Mexico is today. Mexico and the U.S. both have equalization and adjustment lessons to learn from their small island neighbor.

SOCIAL EQUITY CONCERNS

To reap the full benefits of equalization and adjustment, we must consider the issue of social equity. Latin American economies must become more competitive. To achieve this, we will have to attract foreign investment and gain access to technology. In the process of adjusting to these new realities, however, we must avoid hurting the poor. The poor have already borne the brunt of the austerity measures of the 1980s, and we must now move to adjustment based on social equity.

Devaluing currencies, for example, makes Latin American wages attractive to foreign investors, but at the cost of impoverishing workers. This is not the kind of competitiveness we need. Latin America has been trying on its own to become more competitive in other ways. To this end, many countries have encouraged competition by unilaterally lowering trade barriers without expecting reciprocity. In fact, the only current proposal offering reciprocity to Latin Americans is the Enterprise for the Americas Initiative. Neither Japan nor the European Community (EC) have offered to enter into such a free trade agreement with Latin America.

With the reciprocal opening of free trade agreements, competitiveness based on social equity requires that we train labor forces in skills that will attract foreign investment. These better trained laborers will, in turn, have access to better salaries, which will improve income distribution.

NAFTA's ACCESSION CLAUSE

My third point is that this increased efficiency, competition, and trade must be part of an open process of liberalization. We are fortunate that the accession clause in the NAFTA does not exclude nonregional members. Such an exclusion would have been reminiscent of the Monroe Doctrine and could have had disastrous results.

For example, one of the components of the Enterprise for the Americas Initiative provides for the creation of a multilateral investment fund at the Inter-American Development Bank. Japan is a member of the fund and has pledged $500 million, the same amount as the U.S. Imagine if, after accepting Japan's contribution, a clause was included that said Japan was simply not invited to trade with this region. Such an action would have alienated a valuable trading partner and is clearly unreasonable.

Particularly in Latin America, there exists the conviction that a closed accession clause would be detrimental to the development of the hemisphere's nations. In fact, the accession clause is open today specifically at the request of the Mexican delegation. An open clause provides for the possibility that Japan, the EC, or even Korea might come forward with a proposal for a free trade agreement acceptable to Latin America.

In summary, we must include three basic issues in our discussions of the NAFTA: (1) the dynamic gains such as investment must be accompanied by (2) a process of adjustment that contributes to overcoming poverty in the hemisphere through changing productive patterns based on social equity through (3) an open trade liberalization process.

If we take advantage of the NAFTA's dynamic benefits, strive to create adjustments that are fair and equitable, and maintain an open accession clause, I believe we can create a free trade agreement in which everyone wins.

5. The NAFTA and Downward Wage Pressure

by Richard Rothstein

For the past several years, the academic economic establishment in the United States has ignored an important fact about the NAFTA. Usually our economic scholars hold the concept of equilibrium in the highest regard. It has served as the scripture for describing virtually every economic phenomenon. However, many economists have neglected to apply this principle to the integration of the U.S. and Mexican economies through the NAFTA. At President Clinton's economic summit, he and the participants continually reiterated their desire to create a high-wage, high-skill economy in the U.S. In my opinion, it is impossible to integrate a high-wage, high-skill economy with a low-wage economy while hoping to maintain the former at its current wage levels.

Of course, the U.S. has had experience with integrating regions at different levels of development. In the early part of this century, there was a great deal of concern that the flight of manufacturing from higher wage regions in New England and the Northeast to lower wage regions in the Southeast would lead to deterioration of the Northeast. In response, the Roosevelt administration adopted the Fair Labor Standards Act, whose purpose was not to prevent relocation entirely, but to moderate it by establishing common minimum standards. The act also recognized that we could not use purchasing power as an engine for growth if the benefits of industrialization and productivity were not shared more equitably among those producing manufactured goods. One purpose of the act was to raise wages so that workers would have the purchasing power to consume the products that they produced.

One reason we fell into the Depression was that the U.S. had the kind of income distribution in the 1920s that Mexico has today. Workers were producers only and not consumers. In the absence of consumption, production levels could not be sustained.

MEXICAN WAGES

By any standard, Mexican wage levels are currently too low. Although minimum wage levels may be determined by calculations that are, to some extent, arbitrary, that should not excuse us from beginning the discussion of a higher Mexican minimum wage. I am confident that the Clinton administration will initiate that discussion because, as mentioned, it is impossible to achieve our objective while attempting to integrate with a low-wage economy. Even in the U.S., the precise minimum wage level is a somewhat arbitrary compromise between advocates of consumption and production. Nonetheless, we have made that compromise.

PROBLEMS OF WAGE INTEGRATION

There are a number of indicators that suggest Mexican wages are too low for successful integration with the U.S. economy. For one, hourly productivity in Mexico's export sectors is, in many cases, identical to if not higher than that in the U.S. Yet wages are 15 percent of those in this country. Another important indicator is the value added in manufacturing. In Mexico, wages now comprise about 20 percent of manufacturing value added. In the U.S., the figure is 35 percent. Furthermore, we should look at the manner in which national income is distributed between profits, interest, proprietary income, and wages. In the U.S., wages represent about 55 percent of our national income. In Mexico, the comparable figure is only 15 percent.

In the new NAFTA negotiations, we cannot simply dance around the issue of labor standards. Mexican wages are now too low, and an agreement on a new Mexican minimum wage must be reached.

I do not believe this is an inappropriate intervention into Mexican domestic affairs. Wages in Mexico have declined during the past decade between 40 and 50 percent. This decline is not a natural economic phenomenon. It is the result of policy interventions orchestrated by international financial institutions and the U.S. Treasury as part of our structural adjustment plan for Mexico. Its purpose was to reduce wages so that the incomes of Mexican export industries could be devoted primarily to debt service and not to consumption. That type of intervention can and must be reversed if we intend to integrate our economies in anything other than a low-wage direction.

THE PUERTO RICAN EXAMPLE

Let us talk about Puerto Rico, in response to those who jump to the conclusion that a dramatic increase in the Mexican minimum wage will automatically lead to a slowdown in growth.

Over the past several decades, the U.S. Commonwealth of Puerto Rico has developed as part of an integrated U.S. economic system. While there is some dispute over what the tradeoffs have been, Puerto Rico's minimum wage reached U.S. levels in 1981. In the 11 years since achieving equivalency, the island has managed to sustain a per capita income growth of over 3 percent per year. At the same time, Mexico has maintained an annual per capita income growth rate of negative 1 percent.

In fact, if the Mexican wage level was increased, this rate of income growth could be improved. Increased income for the minimum wage-earning sector in Mexico would fuel economic growth by opening up additional domestic markets. The main benefit of integration for the U.S. economy predicted by the Bush administration is the potential market of 80 million Mexican consumers. But that market simply will not have the economic capacity to consume much of what the U.S. and Mexico produce if wages remain at their present level. Unless wages are increased in Mexico, the U.S. will be unable to develop a high-wage, high-skill economy and Mexico will be incapable of achieving the balanced growth that we all hope it will experience.

REMEDIES FOR MEXICO

As a final point, our international experience shows that democratization requires a stable and growing middle class. It is inconceivable that a democratic society can be developed in Mexico with the kind of income distribution existing today. Long-term stability requires more equitable income distribution. In fact, it is remarkable that Mexico has been able to avoid tremendous social upheaval caused by the 50 percent reduction in living standards during the past decade. The only reason I believe it was able to avoid this tumult is because, in spite of regular "elections," Mexico remains an authoritarian country.

When Ross Perot, Paul Tsongas, or Warren Rudman suggested during the U.S. presidential elections a 50 cent-a-gallon gasoline tax to reduce the federal deficit, they confronted a popular wisdom that no democratic leader could ask Americans to accept that kind of suffering and still be elected to office. However, the financial pain withstood by the Mexican people in the past decade has been greater than anything our politicians have suggested we go through ourselves.

6. Dynamic Integration, Foreign Investment, and Open Regionalism in the NAFTA and the Americas

by Van R. Whiting, Jr.

INTRODUCTION

Consider the geopolitical landscape of the world at the start of the 1980s. The world was dominated by a political division between East and West, locked in a Cold War struggle of liberal Western democracies against communism. The developing countries, if not directly involved in this political-military conflict, were engaged in their own struggle for economic development. The dominant theory guiding development policy in Latin America since the 1950s was import substitution under the guiding hand of the state. The United States was the dominant power not only geopolitically but economically as well. U.S. multinational firms were extending their "global reach" and buttressing the position of the United States as a financial and industrial power. Economic liberalism was seen as a theory supported in the North and resisted in the South, with few exceptions. Statism was widely seen as the only recourse of developing countries against dependency.

By the early 1990s, import substitution and the extensive intervention of the state in productive activity had been devalued in theory and in practice as the result of a series of policy failures and crises. Rather than building self-sufficient national economies, import substitution had allowed the selective entry of foreign investment behind protectionist walls, to partake of oligopoly rents in concentrated industries. The absence of a local source of savings led to excessive borrowing from international lenders and a debt crisis that threw Latin America into its worst period of stagnation since the Great Depression. The attempt to regulate the transfer of technology resulted in a reliance on inefficient and outmoded techniques.

In the industrial North, competition intensified. Far from dominating the world economy, the United States itself moved from the position of net creditor to massive debtor. In industries central to the process of industrialization, such as automobiles and electronics, the United States found itself losing market share to firms from Europe and increasingly from Asia. European and Japanese competitors brought products with more adaptable designs, lower cost, and higher quality.

In countries such as Chile and Mexico, economic liberals came to lead development policy, and liberalization and economic cooperation became a demand of these "southern liberals."

As the countries of Latin America consider facing a NAFTA of three plus bilateral trade agreements with Mexico (a de facto Mexico hub-and-spoke), they also are considering subregional free trade groupings of various stripes (CACM, CARICOM, ANCOM, G-3, MERCOSUR) and the possibility of unilateral opening with the world.

In this chapter, I offer an argument to explain the rise of economic liberalization and regional integration in the Americas. The argument comes in three parts. First, geography provides an important basis for functional integration and for comparative advantage. The geopolitical reality of the countries of the Americas varies widely. The intensity of transactions and of information flows between Mexico and the United States is important in understanding the emergence of the NAFTA and why Mexico will receive preferential access to the United States under the NAFTA. This perspective draws on a large literature on functional interdependence and transaction analysis as the basis for integration.

Second, new patterns of foreign investment and the competitive restructuring of international industry present a new set of opportunities for insertion into the world economy as competitors in industrial production and trade. This current restructuring points toward a production zone in North America and a separate production zone in South America. This argument emphasizes industrial organization and location theory: where will global investors locate their plants?

Third, coalition theory is about the intersection of interests and ideas. The emergence of liberalizing coalitions has advanced most in Mexico and Chile. In other countries, powerful interests still defend protectionism; intra-regional transactions are fewer; and information about the global economy is harder to come by. The debate is still broadly engaged across the political spectrum and the conditions for certainty in policy are not yet in place. Regional integration, to be successful, requires at minimum a coalition able to provide predictability in policy, with the institutional and political insulation from specific interests that stability requires. An emerging liberal consensus nevertheless reflects significant differences, reflecting the diversity of opinion and political realities in the Americas. The conclusions recommend as a general prescription stable and predictable policies for open trade and investment policy.

SOCIETAL INTERDEPENDENCE AND REGIONAL INTEGRATION

Trade theory tells us that comparative advantage will bring mutual benefits from liberalization of trade. Only infrequently is geography or location indicated as a comparative advantage, and yet it is clearly so in the case of Mexico. For many years, Mexico's position next to the United States was considered its greatest liability. Now that proximity has become an advantage. Geopolitics, the importance of international strategic and military alliances during the period of the Cold War, has been replaced by geo-economics, the potential comparative advantage from resource endowments, size, and location. In an era of economic competition in a multipolar world, enhancing economic competitiveness is a strategic imperative.

The geopolitical importance of trade efficiency within continental regions is not a recent discovery. Halford J. Mackinder, one of the leading twentieth century proponents of geopolitics, in his 1904 essay, "The Geographical Pivot of History," points out the efficiency gains from the integration of continental powers. "Ocean going traffic, however relatively cheap, usually involves the fourfold handling of goods—at the factory of origin, at the export wharf, at the import wharf, and at the inland warehouse for retail distribution; whereas the continental railway truck may run direct from the exporting factory into the importing warehouse." The tremendous excitement in Europe over the single economic market anticipates precisely these sorts of gains on that continent, and the NAFTA will eventually provide an integrated continental market for Mexico, the United States, and Canada. In the past, the Mexican border might as well have been an ocean; in an integrated market, manufacturing in Mexico may eventually compete from the inside of a continental, land-transport market. The point is not lost on automobile manufacturers, whether Japanese, European, or American.

The importance of manufactured exports (about which more below) for Latin America and the impact of location on investment are highlighted by the declining value of natural resources. Indeed, when we consider the puzzle of Mexico's reversal of position on free trade over the past 10 years, it is worth noting that in 1980, Mexico was primarily an exporter of oil, a commodity for which no political guarantee of market access was necessary. By 1990, Mexico was exporting a majority of manufactured goods, including electronics, auto parts, and finished automobiles. Such products compete directly with U.S. production, and the incentive for a political guarantee of market access is correspondingly higher.

The value of raw materials, on the other hand, has dropped precipitously. According to the IDB Economic and Social Progress in Latin America 1990 Report, the terms of trade turned sharply against raw material exporters in the 1980s. "The fall in commodity prices during the first half of the 1980s was the largest since the Great Depression. The commodity terms of trade dropped nearly forty percent between 1980 and 1986, as compared with the thirty percent drop between 1929 and 1932. Latin America's terms of trade deteriorated almost continuously during the 1980s, so that by 1989 they were 21 percent below their 1980 level." As the IDB indicates, the weakness of commodities led other Latin American countries besides Mexico to diversify into manufactured goods, and to that extent they have an incentive, like Mexico, to seek a political guarantee for market access, or protection against protection.

Functional interdependence has been quite high between Mexico and the United States compared to other Latin American countries. Consider the variety and intensity of cross-border interactions between the United States and Mexico. Mexico is one of the three largest trading partners of the United States (after Canada and Japan). All the Andean countries together take less than a third as many exports from the United States as does Mexico. On the other side, three quarters of Mexico's exports go to the United States, and that percentage has shown remarkable stability in the course of a century, varying between 60 and 80 percent. In contrast, trade with the United States is barely a majority of total exports in the Andean countries and in CARICOM; they are less than half in Central America; and they do not even represent a plurality in Chile or Argentina.

What is true for goods is also true in other areas. The Mexico-U.S. land border is one of the busiest in the world and, protestations notwithstanding, there is a de facto open border to Mexican labor. Foreign investment has been flowing from the United States into Mexico in high and increasing volume. By most measures, Mexico produced less technology of its own and relied more heavily on technology from its neighbor than most others. Mexico is a major oil supplier to the United States. The two countries have worked closely together on border issues; on controlling the drug trade; on renegotiating the debt; on migration; and on many less sweeping but important issues, from fishing rights to prisoner exchanges. This breadth and intensity of cross-border interaction created a positive environment for a long-term commitment to continued cooperation and facilitated the negotiation of the North American Free Trade Agreement.

The density of issues to be negotiated among Mexico, the U.S., and Canada is reflected in the 19 working groups set up as part of the negotiations. Both Mexico and the United States were able to mount both government-to-government and private sector-to-private sector teams in each of these areas. The well-developed pluralism of the private sector in both countries contributed to the web of interdependence. Thus, the density of issues and the parallel pluralism facilitated greater flows of information, reduced transaction costs, and a greater facility for initiating and pursuing to conclusion a broad-based free trade agreement (FTA).

In contrast to the intensity of interactions among the three countries of North America, none of the subregions of South America come even close to the patterns of functional integration in Europe or in North America. To take a simple measure, intra-regional trade in the 1980s constituted more than 60 percent of total trade in the European Community (EC); intra-regional trade accounted for 38 percent of exports in the NAFTA. Intra-regional trade in Central America was only 10 percent; CARICOM was 6 percent; MERCOSUR was about 4 percent; and the Andean countries' intra-regional trade was only 2.5 percent of their total exports. Thus, the functional demand for integration was higher in the NAFTA countries than in the rest of the hemisphere; the rewards to be reaped from integration are correspondingly higher there.

FOREIGN INVESTMENT AND NEW OPPORTUNITIES

Although the debates about regional integration often appear to be about trade, in fact the more important issues concern the broadening of the liberal international regime to cover flows in the factors of production—or at least those in which the United States is surplus. (Labor flows are not being discussed directly in the General Agreement on Tariffs and Trade or in the NAFTA.) However, just as the "new areas" in GATT are trade related investment measures (TRIMs), intellectual property (TRIPs), and services, so too these factor flows are crucial to the interests of the United States in consolidating free trade arrangements with Mexico and throughout the Americas.

Let us look briefly at the ways in which foreign investment has evolved in Latin America in the twentieth century. I argue that we are witnessing a third wave of competitive restructuring of global industry, with significant consequences for investment patterns in the Americas.

As background, we may recall that the United States initially satisfied the Latin American market for manufactures by means of exports, just as Japan initially shipped their cars to America fully assembled. In the first wave of foreign direct investment in Latin America, the countries of the region raised tariff and nontariff barriers to imports. The foreign investors "jumped" the tariff barriers and established themselves comfortably as protected oligopolies producing for the local market with the protection of the state. Import substitution industrialization thus protected multinationals as well as domestic firms, and the inefficiencies of that system affected both.

As European and especially Asian competition began to penetrate U.S. markets, the competitive response of U.S. firms produced a second wave of investment, often referred to as the internationalization of production. The Maquiladoras coexisted under a separate free trade arrangement with protected import-substituting investment. The idea of internationalized production or offshore assembly was to split off the labor-intensive portion of manufacturing and locate that production in a low-wage country. Mexican maquilas grew steadily from their initial establishment in 1965, growing right through the otherwise stagnant decade of the 1980s; by 1990, more than 2,000 plants had been established and nearly half a million workers were employed. This level of offshore assembly investment in Mexico dwarfs by far the amount of maquila employment in the Dominican Republic or in Central America.

The establishment of a NAFTA will eliminate the distinction between maquilas and foreign investment for the local market. The increased security of investors in Mexico under a NAFTA may provide even greater incentive to locate maquila production there; this is certainly a worry of Central American and Caribbean assembly operators. However, a counter-trend may eventually favor the Central American and Caribbean offshore plants. The integration of Mexico into the NAFTA will surely have the effect of raising wages in Mexico. Therefore, there will increasingly be a tradeoff between the need for geographical proximity and the availability of low-wage labor. A likely outcome will be an increase in investment in Mexico in heavy equipment or component sectors (such as automobiles or televisions) for which transportation is an important cost. In contrast, Mexico will become less competitive in easily transportable low-wage maquila production.

The third wave of global restructuring (following import-substituting and maquila investments) may be termed "integrated regional production." Such production is growing in Mexico, where the automobile industry includes not only parts and components but also engines and finished vehicles for export to the U.S. market. What is the dynamic behind this new pattern of investment? The answer reveals the incentive of the United States for regional integration. It also reveals the protectionist dimension of regionalization. As North-North industrial competition intensified, with European and Japanese producers competing for market share with U.S. firms in their home market, those firms sought an even greater competitive response than the maquilas provided. As I have argued elsewhere, it is not so much the case that free trade will bring in new investment. Rather, investment in Mexico in the 1980s, by Ford, IBM, Sony, Volkswagen, and many others, represented an investment response to Mexico's liberalization. Regional integration initiatives followed rather than lead liberalized trade and investment policy.

Nevertheless, the negotiation of the NAFTA will provide an import-substituting protection to North American manufacturers. By means of rules of origin (62.5 percent in the case of automobiles), Japanese manufacturers shipping from Japan would either lose their cost advantage or face an incentive to relocate their production to North America. This is a classic example of import substitution policy using local content rules.

Given the importance of proximity for integrated regional production, North American integration has a production logic that is unique. The production efficiency of South America through MERCOSUR is analogous. The efficiency gains will be achieved by the elimination of intra-continental trade barriers in South America; producers from Europe, North America, and Asia will locate production there for an expanded South American regional market. It is unlikely that South American manufacturing will become part of a hemispheric integrated regional production strategy.

This does not mean, however, that there is no possibility of manufactured exports to the United States from countries other than Mexico. If integrated regional production is one part of North-South competition, "flexible specialization" is the other part. This means that specialized products with small worldwide demand can be produced efficiently in any open economy and shipped globally, gaining economies of scale and low-wage advantages. As Juan Falconi articulated the strategy for Ecuador, those countries that aggressively seek foreign investment will gain an advantage in trade. Countries that are not part of a triad market will nevertheless be able to liberalize on the basis of natural comparative advantage. Chile's export gains are real, but are closer to the traditional specification of comparative advantage than to the integrated regional production of industrial investments in Mexico's north.

The new industrial organization and location theory provide an alternative to traditional international trade theory, as Paul Krugman has demonstrated. What are the implications for industry and for governments? For industry, as liberalization proceeds, firms will be expected to meet international standards of efficiency and competitiveness. This means, as U.S. firms are trying to learn and as Latin American firms will have to: 1) low-cost production along the entire productive chain; 2) total quality in production, in marketing, and in service; and 3) just-in-time production.

The implication of industrial organization and location theory is that international economic cooperation will ensure opportunities for investment and technology for U.S. firms, while providing assured market access in the U.S. for Latin America. Location of production by investors is as central to the process as is the destination of goods or the barriers to trade.

The new industrial organization does not mean a minimal role for the state, but it does imply a very different role, from protecting producers to protecting consumers and providing public goods in the form of human and physical infrastructure. The state will no longer be engaged directly in productive activities; privatization will proceed apace. The new state role will be to provide essential oversight functions to assure a level playing field to prevent abuses, without unduly increasing the regulatory burden; to provide the training of human resources necessary for internationally competitive production; and to modernize the infrastructure for transportation and communications required by globally efficient firms. This new agenda for the state means breaking the old alliances built and supported by import substitution policies and creating a new liberalizing coalition.

LIBERAL COALITIONS, REGIONALISTS, AND GLOBALISTS

The current literature on economic cooperation in the Americas has taken the form of an argument about how to expand the coverage of the North American free trade area beyond Canada, the United States, and Mexico to include the rest of the countries of the Americas and possibly expand into Asia. The debate has focused on the prior conditions that Latin American countries should fulfill to be eligible for inclusion in an expanded NAFTA, and the form that expansion should take: a "hub-and-spoke" system in which the United States serves as the hub of a trading area and signs free trade agreements with the countries of the region (the spokes), or alternatively the accession of Latin American countries to the NAFTA once it is formed. It now seems clear that this debate has been superseded by the dynamic of North American integration. Once the NAFTA is formed, Mexico and Canada will want to be party to U.S. trade negotiations with other countries of the Americas. In the meantime, Mexico has pursued a bilateral policy of free trade with other countries of the Americas. De facto, the short-term reality will be a North American free trade area, with the eventual possibility of accession over the long run by the other countries, and a "Mexico Hub" in which Mexico has free trade with the United States and Canada, on the one hand, and with a series of Latin American countries, on the other. Thus, the most likely outcome in the short run, though the least desirable from the perspective of the rest of the hemisphere, is the NAFTA plus the Mexico Hub.

But liberalizing coalitions are arising throughout the Americas; as a consensus emerges about the necessity of economic liberalization, debates are being formed about subregional versus global opening. Let me briefly explore the basis of liberalizing coalitions and the emerging consensus and "dissensus".

Some attribute economic liberalization to liberal leadership. There is an element of truth in this; Salinas studied political economy at Harvard, while Echeverría and López Portillo studied law at UNAM. However, liberalizing coalitions are more likely where old alliances are weakening or declining and where shifting interests create the basis for new alliances. The coalition supporting import substitution has been strong and well entrenched. At its heart it is a producer alliance supporting a policy that generated concentrated benefits and imposed its costs on a broad and unorganized group of consumers, justified by politicians using populist and nationalist rhetoric. Import substitution did allow some infant industries to survive and grow. But the heart of the policy was protected producers, protected economic sectors, and protected government bureaucracies. To these beneficiaries were added those able to use side payments to obtain special favors and monopoly rents that protection made possible.

The logic of nationalism under import substitution was to maximize local production for the local market. The inward-looking coalition began to come apart in the 1980s for several reasons. First, import substitution began to fail in its own terms: it was unable to mobilize savings domestically, it was unable to produce technology domestically, and it was unable to produce a sufficient number of jobs for workers and consumer markets for producers. With the stagnation of domestic markets in Latin

America in the aftermath of the debt crisis, manufacturers who had long benefited from import substitution and had grown with the national market realized that they would have to seek external markets in order to continue and sustain growth. In addition, consumers as well as enterprises became more aware, through improved information flows, of prices and quality of consumer goods and capital goods in international markets. Although this seldom produced a coherent lobby in favor of liberalization, it did produce a black market in world-class products that represented significant leakage of protection and produced frustrated aspirations on the part of consumers.

It becomes possible then to see the shape of a new liberalizing coalition. Growth-oriented firms seek expanded domestic markets, including those served by their protected competitors or by state enterprises. Firms with the capacity to export want liberalized raw materials, intermediate goods, and capital goods for their industries and are willing to accept import competition in order to achieve export efficiency. Access to world-class information technology, including hardware, software, and telecommunications, becomes essential for firms seeking to expand their markets.

For governments, the realization that import substitution did not buy political success led to a greater willingness to experiment with alternative solutions. The key to this alchemy (and the political genius of Carlos Salinas in Mexico) is to transform the definition of nationalism from maximizing the local production for the local market into maximizing the nation's share of the global market. This outward-looking nationalist vision makes it possible to mobilize support for liberalization. Once the gains from trade are seen, a broad liberalizing coalition can be formed, as in Mexico and in Chile.

The political lesson from trade coalition analysis is that scarce factors of production are protected under import substitution and are threatened by free trade. However, scarcity is not necessarily defined vis-à-vis the global market; it must be defined vis-à-vis major trading partners. Mexico, like the United States, is land-rich compared to the rest of the world and could export agricultural products to Europe and Japan. However, vis-à-vis the United States, Mexico is labor-rich. Therefore, in agricultural trade, post-NAFTA, labor-intensive agriculture will gain in Mexico while land-intensive exports will flourish in the United States. The relative endowments of factors specific to sector and trading partner will determine winners and losers.

Using this shorthand—that scarce factors lose and abundant factors win in specific sector/country relations under conditions of free trade—makes it possible to predict winners and losers from liberalized trade among any set of trade partners. The political challenge is to structure a policy alliance that can survive the opposition of formerly protected producers long enough for the gains from trade to begin to be realized and long enough to provide a planning horizon for investors and producers.

In research conducted throughout the Americas during 1991 and 1992, I found, among specialists in the area, elements of consensus and dissensus regarding regional integration. Interviews were conducted with private and government officials in six countries and a set of statements were developed representing the range of the debate. Approximately 40 experts were then asked to rank the statements.

The elements of agreement are significant. There is general agreement that regional integration is driven by the desire to "protect against protection" in the U.S. and that the extension of integration efforts is a response to Mexican competition with the advent of the NAFTA. There is also agreement that the process is a gradual one. On the negative side, there is general disagreement that opening must take place among equals—an old tenet of integration theory. Most of the respondents also disagreed that the U.S. valued GATT more than its relations with Mexico and the Americas, showing significant skepticism about U.S. multilateral leadership.

Beyond the consensus, disagreements emerged between globalists, who see regional integration as a step (perhaps second-best) toward an open world, and regionalists, who see new regional and subregional groups as desirable in themselves. The globalists hold that free trade is important and that opening with neighbors, with the region, and with the world can be compatible. They strongly support the statement that "free trade is important for us, both to consolidate a national strategy for competitiveness and to provide a longer time horizon with stable rules of the game."

Some points significantly separate the globalists from the regionalists. The global liberals see macroeconomic opening as more important than trade agreements and hold that "the optimal policy would be to open with the world." The globalists disagree that Mexico should enjoy a long transition, that small countries lose from opening, and that negotiating with the U.S. could be devastating. They are also anxious to get going, without waiting for lengthy studies. On all these points, the globalists are polarized from the regionalists.

The regionalists want to integrate first with their neighbors, then bargain with the U.S. as a group; G-3, Mercosur, and the Andean group are important steps for these specialists. Subregional groupings are seen to have greater bargaining power. They see no necessary connection between opening with one country and opening with the world. They strongly disagree with the statement that "the opening is more important than the winners and losers." For them, regionalism has value of its own, not only because it is a route to global opening.

These interviews show that liberalization is sweeping the Americas. One-country nationalism is out. But significant differences remain about the pace and the partners most likely to produce the most gains.

CONCLUSIONS: DYNAMIC GAINS FROM OPEN REGIONS

In order to successfully liberalize, governments need to provide predictability and certainty over the medium term. This in turn requires the ability to insulate government from the pressures of protected producers. Policy stability and autonomy require strong political leadership and a strong party system. Although liberalization does not require democracy, the conditions for sustained liberalization are also the conditions for the institutionalization of democracy.

PART III

IMPLICATIONS OF THE NAFTA FOR DEVELOPMENT

7. The Rocky Road toward Hemispheric Economic Integration: A Regional Background with Attention to the Future

by Joseph Grunwald

The Western Hemisphere has arrived at an ironic juncture. The United States, for many years the champion of multilateralism and promoter of global free trade, is now pushing regionalism. Latin American countries, for many years limited by import-substituting industrialization and failed regional economic integration efforts, have finally moved toward opening their economies to the world, but they now find themselves tempted by a U.S. initiative to join a regional trading bloc. An additional irony is that Latin American countries' past attempts to band together in various kinds of economic union were usually efforts to make the region less dependent on the United States. Most Latin American countries now seem eager to join the United States in free trade arrangements.

THE HISTORICAL SETTING

Until very recently, the image of Latin America was that of stagnating economies laboring inefficiently behind high trade walls erected to promote domestic industrialization. Within a broad historical context, that impression was valid for only a brief time. Even then, this did not truly reflect reality, given that between the 1950s and 1970s many Latin American countries' growth rates were among the highest in the world.

The original version of this article was written for publication in THE ENTERPRISE FOR THE AMERICAS INITIATIVE, Roy E. Green, ed. (Praeger Publishers, an imprint of Greenwood Publishing Group, Westport, CT, forthcoming late 1993).

For most of Latin America's history, free trade prevailed over protectionism. Through the colonial period and other stages of "informal" European imperialism, Latin American countries were viewed as export economies dedicated to the sale of their natural resources overseas. Before the end of the 19th century, the United States began to replace Europe as the principal source of capital, and the free exchange of Latin American primary commodities for American manufactured goods became the basis of U.S. economic power in the region.

Under the hegemony of Europe and, more recently, of the United States, local Latin American economic interests benefited and cooperated with outside powers to preserve conditions advantageous to international commerce. Since the time that its citizens initiated significant economic relations with the region in the second half of the 19th century and until the early post-war period, "the United States continued to see the Latin American republics as simple agrarian countries and producers of raw materials for export [and importers of manufactures] even while Latin America turned toward industrialization."[1] This encouraged the economic expansion of both the United States and local Latin American elites.

Inter-American relations changed during the post-World War II period, as major Latin American countries seriously embarked on import substituting industrialization. However, after supplying strategic raw materials (at set prices) to the United States in return for production assistance (primarily through the Export-Import Bank) to regional economies, the intense wartime economic cooperation gave way to a period of disappointment for Latin America. Aid to the region dried up as the United States focused on Europe and the world economy, and U.S. private business interests and U.S. officials expressed their strong distaste for Latin American import substitution policies of trade restriction and state intervention. The United States lectured Latin America on the benefits of free private enterprise, while U.S. manufacturers discovered that they could prosper by setting up subsidiaries in the region behind high trade barriers.

THE WESTERN HEMISPHERE IDEA

Geography and history, reinforced by economic and political considerations, have often stimulated a special relationship between the United States and Latin America. The "Western Hemisphere idea" emerged in the 1880s as a counterweight against the strong and growing European influence in Latin America.[2] An early highlight of Pan-Americanism was the First International

Conference of American States, held in Washington, D.C., during the winter of 1889-90. The conference's agenda included not only the creation of an American customs union, but also the establishment of regular communications between American ports, a Pan American railway, a system of customs regulations, standard weights and measures, laws to protect copyrights and trademarks, and a common silver coin.[3]

However, the conference failed to construct a continental customs union. The opposition was led by Argentina, which held close economic ties to Europe. Other countries in Latin America, possibly anticipating an eventual desire to advance their own industrialization, showed little support for the scheme. Growing protectionist sentiment in the United States, culminating in the 1890 McKinley Tariff Act, dampened enthusiasm for a continental customs union. The Western Hemisphere idea has waxed and waned in irregular cycles since these experiments in the late 1800s.

At the Second International Conference of American States held in Mexico City in 1901-02, the idea of a continental customs union was not presented. With a few exceptions, notably U.S. Secretary of State Cordell Hull's tariff-cutting proposal for increasing hemispheric trade at the Seventh International Conference of American States in 1933, economic integration did not play a positive role in inter-American policy until the 1961 Alliance for Progress.

THE ALLIANCE FOR PROGRESS

The Alliance was referred to as "the renascence of the Western Hemisphere idea . . . for a few brief years, that program represented the apparent triumph of Pan-Americanism."[4] The Alliance flagged for various reasons soon after it was established. First, Latin American countries did not take seriously the Alliance's call for reform in areas such as land holding, tax, education, and administration. Latin American policymakers knew that the fundamental motivation for the U.S. initiative was the emerging threat of Castro's Cuba and the fear of Soviet penetration into the hemisphere, and most countries correctly surmised that financial assistance was predicated on that conflict rather than their own attempts at economic reform. (They did meet another condition for aid, the preparation of nonbinding economic and social development plans, easily formulated with the help of contracted foreign econometricians.)

The 1967 Punta del Este summit meeting of heads of state in the Americas was promoted with great fanfare by U.S. President Lyndon B. Johnson. To encourage Latin American economic integration, President Johnson offered financial support for a Latin American Common Market, but his request for a $1.5 billion five-year aid commitment was not supported by the U.S. Congress. (Interestingly, the $1.5 billion offered in 1967 was, in 1990 dollars, about four times as much as the $1.5 billion fund created under the 1990 Enterprise for the Americas Initiative [EAI]). Although the summit was hemisphere-wide, the United States, as the world's main defender of multilateralism, did not propose to be included in the Common Market.[5]

The summit elation soon fizzled. Fear of balance of payments losses was not overcome by any concrete offer of U.S. aid, and, perhaps more importantly, the specter of domination by external private investors emerged as a strong hindrance to Latin American integration. Suddenly it appeared that a Latin American Common Market might be highly vulnerable to economic penetration by the United States. The early experience of the European Economic Community (EC) showed that subsidiaries of giant U.S. international corporations in Europe had grown faster than European firms.[6]

Latin American apprehensions were aggravated by unilateral U.S. economic moves, such as the withholding of aid to Peru during that country's dispute with a U.S. oil company in the early 1960s, and the 1962 Hickenlooper amendment to the U.S. foreign assistance and sugar acts. This and other similar congressional commercial restrictions "were inevitably seen in Latin America as forms of economic coercion: they seemed to give foreign investors decisive status in determining the legitimacy of policies followed by sovereign states."[7]

GLOBALISM

By the 1970s, the United States was again emphasizing global interdependence; Latin America played a relatively small role in U.S. foreign trade compared to Europe, East Asia, and Canada (Table 1). Thus, Latin America was put on the back burner in U.S. foreign policy. Policies implying that "no special privilege can be conceded to Latin America because equally important interests elsewhere in the world would be adversely affected"[8] remained until President Bush's declaration of regional interdependence in the 1990 Enterprise for the Americas Initiative.

On the Latin American side, trade with the United States as a percentage of total trade had declined for most countries since the early post-war period (Table 2). Nevertheless, the United

TABLE 1

U.S. Trade with Latin America as a Percentage of Total U.S. Trade (Various Years), 1950-91

	U.S. Exports to Latin America as % of Total U.S. Exports	U.S. Imports from Latin America as % of Total U.S. Imports
1950	28%	35%
1958-59	23	28
1963-65	16	21
1974-76	14	12
1979-81	17	14
1984-86	14	13
1989-91	14	13

Note: The International Monetary Fund changed the definition of Latin America, starting with the 1985 Yearbook of *Direction of International Trade Statistics*, affecting post-1977 data. After 1977, "Latin America" conforms to the IMF definition of "Western Hemisphere," all of the Western Hemisphere less the United States, Canada, and Cuba. The percentages calculated on the basis of the new series for the last three rows in the table are about two points higher compared to the previous definitions. Thus, the 1979-81 average Latin American share is 15 percent of U.S. exports and 12 percent of U.S. imports calculated on the basis of the old series.

Sources: For 1950: A. Fishlow, "The Mature Neighbor Policy," in J. Grunwald, ed., *Latin America and World Economy* (Beverly Hills, CA: Sage Publications, 1978), Table 4.1, p. 38. For 1958-1976: *Direction of Trade Annual 1958-62*, *Annual 1963-67*, and *Annual 1970-76* (Washington, D.C.: Joint Publications of the International Monetary Fund and the International Bank for Reconstruction and Development, 1963 and 1967). For 1979-91: *Direction of Trade Statistics, Yearbooks 1985, 1991*, and *1992* (Washington, D.C.: International Monetary Fund, 1985, 1991, and 1992).

States has remained the most important trading partner for most countries in the region.

LATIN AMERICAN ECONOMIC INTEGRATION

Despite fervent exhortations by influential Latin American intellectuals and policymakers, the idea of regional economic integration remained rhetorical until the middle of this century. In fact, the Central Latin American Common Market (CACM) and the Latin American Free Trade Association (LAFTA) treaties were not signed until 1960.[9]

TABLE 2

Latin America and Selected Countries: Trade with the United States as a Percentage of Total Trade (Various Years), 1950-91

	Exports to U.S. as % of Total Exports			Imports from U.S. as % of Total Imports		
	1950	1961-65	1989-91	1950	1961-65	1989-91
Latin America*	52%	36%	38%	49%	42%	38%
Argentina	19	8	12	20	25	25
Brazil	54	36	23	35	32	22
Chile	52	35	18	48	38	20
Colombia	82	54	43	70	50	36
Mexico	86	59	72	84	68	69
Peru	26	34	23	53	40	29
Venezuela	56	35	51	69	53	47

* Latin America includes all Latin American countries except Cuba in 1950; for all other years, Latin America includes all of the Western Hemisphere less the United States, Canada, and Cuba (corresponds to the "Western Hemisphere" definition of the IMF for 1989-91, and approximately to the "Latin America" definition of the Inter-American Development Bank for 1961-65).

Source: For 1950: J. Grunwald, M.S. Wionczek, and M. Carnoy, *Latin American Economic Integration and U.S. Policy* (Washington, D.C.: Brookings Institution, 1972), Table A-4, pp. 168-71. For 1961-65: *Annual Report* (Washington, D.C.: Inter-American Development Bank, 1967). For 1989-91: *Direction of Trade Statistics, Yearbook 1992* (Washington, D.C.: International Monetary Fund, 1992).

The Latin American Free Trade Association and Its Successor

Eventually, the LAFTA treaty included the 10 South American countries (Argentina, Bolivia, Brazil, Chile, Colombia, Ecuador, Paraguay, Peru, Uruguay, and Venezuela) and Mexico and provided for the gradual elimination of all intraregional trade barriers within 12 years. At first, hundreds of tariffs were reduced in item by item negotiations, primarily on products in which there was little or no trade among the member countries. LAFTA made less progress in eliminating trade barriers on products in which its members competed. Recognizing failure, in 1980 the partner countries established the Latin American Integration Association (LAIA), superseding LAFTA. Fixed targets, such as yearly tariff reduction commitments, schedules for the freeing of trade by certain percentages, and the common market date were abandoned. LAIA is an informal, open-ended arrangement that has emphasized integration by projects and has not put pressure on the member countries to liberalize their external trade.

The Andean Group

When LAFTA weaknesses became apparent in the mid-1960s, the six Andean countries—Bolivia, Chile, Colombia, Ecuador, Peru, and Venezuela—banded together under LAFTA to form the Andean Subregional Integration Agreement. The original Andean Pact of 1969 was much more ambitious than LAFTA. It provided for the automatic and irrevocable reduction of tariff and nontariff barriers to intra-Andean trade, a common external tariff within 10 years, establishment of sectoral industrial development programs, harmonization and coordination of economic policies and development plans, and a controversial common regime for the treatment of foreign investment and technology.

So far, the Andean Group has not gotten any closer to economic integration than LAFTA did. One of its major achievements has been the establishment of the Andean Development Corporation, CAF, by its Spanish acronym, which functions as a subregional development bank. CAF has contributed to regional investments but has been unable to increase the importance of trade within the zone, the lowest proportion of intra-regional trade of any integration scheme in Latin America (Table 3). Balance-of-payments concerns have been obstacles to progress, as have the similarity of factor endowments and the poor quality of connecting infrastructure among the countries. Chile, the original prime mover of the Pact, withdrew in 1976 as its new military regime liberalized the economy. More recently, the now five-member Andean Group has introduced what it hopes will be more realistic goals toward a common market.

The Central American Common Market

For more than a century, the memory of past bloody struggles and regional prejudices have led to the failure of some three dozen attempts at uniting Central America. The postwar Central American integration movement therefore started from a much lower base of intra-regional commerce than LAFTA (see Table 4). Beginning in 1951, careful preparation of regional economic cooperation under the leadership of the United Nations Economic Commission for Latin America overcame past hostilities, leading to the signing of the common market treaty in 1960.

TABLE 3

Latin America: Share of Intra-regional Exports (Various Years), 1938-90

	Intra-LAIA Export as % of Total	Intra-AND Export as % of Total	Intra-CAC Export as % of Total	Intra-CAR Export as % of Total	Intra-LAT Export as % of Total
1938	6%	na	na	na	6%
1950	8	na	3	na	8
1960	8	1	7	5	8
1970	10	3	27	8	13
1980	14	3	22	9	15
1990	10*	4	15	13*	16

Note: LAIA includes AND, MERCOSUR, Chile, and Mexico; AND: Andean Group; CAC: CACM; CAR: CARIFTA; LAT: All of Latin America and Caribbean; na: not available; *1989.

Memo Items: In 1991, intra-MERCOSUR exports were 9 percent of total MERCOSUR exports, Chile's Latin American exports were 14 percent of its total exports, and Mexican Latin American exports were 4 percent of its total (see last source below).

Source: For 1938: D.W. Baerresen, M. Carnoy, and J. Grunwald, *Latin American Trade Patterns* (Washington, D.C.: Brookings Institution, 1965), Table II-b, p. 76. For Andean Group and CARICOM in 1960: U. Lächler, "Regional Integration and Economic Development" (The World Bank Industry and Energy Department, PPR, Working Paper No. 14, November 1989), Table 7, p. 18. For all others in 1950 and 1960: J. Grunwald, M.S. Wionczek, and M. Carnoy, *Latin American Economic Integration and U.S. Policy* (Washington, D.C.: Brookings Institution, 1972), Table 3, p. 46. For Latin America in 1970 and 1980: *Statistical Yearbook for Latin America and the Caribbean*, 1988 Edition (Santiago, Chile: United Nations Economic Commission for Latin America and the Caribbean, 1989), Tables 287 and 289, pp. 558-559 and 564-565. For all others in 1970, 1980, and 1989: A. Inotai, "Regional Integration among Developing Countries, Revisited" (World Bank, The Policy, Research, and External Affairs Complex, WPS 643, April 1991), Table 2, p. 50. For 1990: J. Nogués and R. Quintanilla, "Latin America's Integration and the Multilateral Trading System" (World Bank and CEPR Conference on New Dimensions in Regional Integration April 2-3, 1992), Table 8, p. 20; and *Direction of Trade Statistics, 1992* (Washington, D.C.: International Monetary Fund, 1992).

Central American intra-regional commerce thrived, due to the closeness of the countries, the low economic disparity between them, compared to LAFTA, and fairly stable macroeconomic conditions. When armed hostilities between El Salvador and Honduras erupted in 1969, intra-regional trade had reached more than one quarter of total CACM trade. In the 1970s, CACM was further weakened by the dissatisfaction of the three lagging partners, Costa Rica, Guatemala, and Honduras, which suspended its membership, and by rising fiscal and balance-of-payments deficits, foreign exchange controls, and declining foreign demand for regional products. In the 1980s, the armed conflicts in Nicaragua and El Salvador destroyed regional economic relations. By 1987, intra-regional exports had fallen to less than 12 percent of total exports. With the end of hostilities, the decline in the debt crisis, and substantial economic reforms, Central America is poised to resume its march toward economic integration.[10]

Other Integration Schemes

MERCOSUR. By far the largest, and also newest, subregional arrangement is the Common Market of the South, MERCOSUR by its Spanish acronym, comprising Argentina, Brazil, Paraguay, and Uruguay. Emerging from bilateral trade agreements between Argentina and Brazil in the mid-1980s, the common market treaty was signed in 1991 and provided for the elimination of all trade barriers between the four countries, common external tariffs, and harmonization of economic policies by mid-decade. Chile, more than half of whose Latin American trade is with Brazil and Argentina, was invited but refused to join because of economic instability and high trade barriers in MERCOSUR countries, particularly Brazil. Since 1991, when intra-MERCOSUR exports were only 9 percent of total MERCOSUR exports (Table 3, Memo Items), Argentina-Brazil trade has surged.

CARICOM. The smallest integration program in the Western Hemisphere is the Caribbean Community (CARICOM). Established in 1972, CARICOM has 13 member countries and looks toward the construction of a common market before the end of this century.[11] Its intra-group trade is still small, although it rose from 5 percent in 1965 to almost 13 percent at the end of the 1980s.

SELA. The Latin American Economic System, SELA by its Spanish acronym, is a promoter of Latin American economic cooperation rather than an integration agreement. It was established in 1975 to "arrange common positions [in international forums] and galvanize cooperation for economic and social progress in the 25 Latin American member countries."[12]

LATIN AMERICAN ECONOMIC INTEGRATION AND THE EAI

An important motivation for Latin American integration in the 1950s was to establish a counterweight against the overwhelming economic power of the United States in the region. Guided by the European integration process, Latin American countries hoped that opening up markets to each other would strengthen their economies vis-à-vis the world economy, especially that of the United States. Economic strength would derive from the expanded benefits of regional, rather than national, import substituting industrialization.

Because of its strong belief in multilateralism, the United States was cool, if not actually opposed, to Latin American economic integration. Regional blocs, particularly among underdeveloped countries, would prevent the optimum allocation of resources. For special reasons, European integration was considered an exception.

U.S. policy changed with the Alliance for Progress. In the East-West struggle, the United States needed a secure hemisphere and rekindled its interest in the region's economic development. The United States became supportive of Latin American economic integration, leading to the 1967 summit.

After subsequent disenchantment with Latin American cooperation efforts and occasional Latin American rebuffs of U.S. overtures, the United States disengaged from regional integration enterprises. It continued to provide some funding to regional institutions such as the Central American Bank for Economic Integration and CAF, not to mention major U.S. support for the Inter-American Development Bank, which financed integration projects.

Despite the depressing failures of regional integration, Latin Americans have never given up the idea of economic union. Integration agreements, although languishing during most of the past three decades, have survived. Stimulated by the debt crisis and its aftermath, the movement toward integration revived at the end of the 1980s. The region undertook bold new initiatives, including the strengthening of common market commitments by all subregional groups and the emergence of MERCOSUR. The newly modified trade agreements are more efficient because Latin American countries have opened their economies, unilaterally reducing trade barriers and bureaucratic obstacles to international commerce.

The possibility that the EAI may provide a more effective impulse to Latin American integration than Latin Americans were able to muster in the past is ironic given that integration was originally conceived in part as a means to increase the region's bargaining power with the United States. The object is no longer to band together to avoid being overwhelmed by the U.S. economy. Several countries have surmised that a real integration stimulus may now come from linking with the U.S. economy, even though the importance of trade relations with the United States has declined since the early postwar period (Table 2). The EAI takes into account the possibility of free trade agreements (FTAs) between subregional integration pacts and the United States.

Just as France and Germany have taken the leadership in the economic union process in Europe, the United States is doing so in the Americas.

WESTERN HEMISPHERE INTEGRATION: PROBLEMS AND PROSPECTS

Because Latin American trade barriers are still much higher than those of the United States, an FTA with the U.S. will require the continuation of unilateral trade liberalization by Latin American partners. Adjustment problems will diminish if Latin American countries and subregional groups liberalize their own trade regimes before negotiating FTAs with the United States.

Integration Fears and Objectives

During the earlier period of intra-Latin American integration, the principal obstacle was the fear of de-industrialization and of balance-of-payments losses. Most members of integration agreements perceived dangers in lowering trade barriers. If domestic industries are not competitive, the country might be flooded with imports, bankrupting many firms and causing a deterioration of the balance of payments. This scenario would be aggravated by a loss of exports. Furthermore, imports might be diverted from lower cost extra-regional suppliers to higher cost intra-regional producers.[13]

Grounds for these fears have grown weaker. Combined with other economic reforms in most Latin American countries, unilateral trade liberalization has eliminated grossly inefficient firms, and international competitiveness has increased. Armed with these improvements, Latin American countries still prefer to trade with developed industrial countries rather than with each other. In addition to the high technology available in developed countries, these firms can derive significant practical advantages from dealing with exporters and importers in those nations. For instance, they may obtain supplier credits that most often are not available from other Latin American countries.[14]

Most Latin American nations, excluding the largest oil producers, Mexico and Venezuela, still trade predominantly with countries outside the Western Hemisphere (compare Tables 2 and 3). This has led to a fear of high trade diversion costs for Latin American countries joining an FTA with the United States. Yet, trade diversion is not considered terribly relevant in Latin America; such costs are viewed as short term in nature and a reasonable price to pay for long-term benefits.

The immediate goal of joining an FTA with the United States is not trade expansion but the bolstering of foreign and domestic confidence in Latin American economies. Increased confidence may lead to increased foreign and domestic resources for badly needed infrastructure. When transportation and communications improve and the labor force is upgraded through effective education and training, private investment can thrive. After new investments bear fruit, exports will expand vigorously. This reasoning may explain Mexico's willingness to accept the significant costs of trade diversion possible under the NAFTA's severe rules of origin demanded by the United States.

While trade diversion may not greatly worry Latin American countries contemplating an FTA with the United States, investment diversion is a serious concern. For example, the NAFTA may attract investments to Mexico at the expense of Caribbean basin countries or Brazil. Apprehension over losing investments are more real than balance-of-payments considerations, which seem to have receded into the background.[15]

FTA Expansion

Countries excluded from an FTA with the United States may suffer from investment diversion, but late comers to an agreement are assumed to be at a disadvantage as well. Moreover, the benefits of joining early could be diluted upon the entry of new members. If Latin American countries accede to the NAFTA, will it weaken or strengthen Mexico's position?

If trade were the only issue involved, then accession to the NAFTA would benefit both Mexico and the new member, provided that NAFTA's trade with the outside world does not diminish.[16]

But, as indicated earlier, Mexico's immediate FTA goal is confidence building. It is not clear whether a NAFTA expansion will enhance or weaken Mexico's potential for attracting resources. Multiple FTAs between individual countries or regional blocs and the United States—a "hub and spoke" system—could create competition between the FTAs for investment and other resources, possibly lowering net Latin American benefits. A hub-and-spoke system would be less efficient than one comprehensive agreement because in the former, trade barriers would persist between individual FTAs.[17]

Asymmetry

Prior to the NAFTA, all formal economic integration arrangements in Europe, Africa, Asia, and Latin America were negotiated between countries at similar levels of development. While there was a significant difference in per capita income between Italy and France in the 1950s when the EC was formed, or between Paraguay and Argentina in 1960 when the original LAFTA agreement was signed, the huge gap between Mexican and U.S. income levels is significantly greater.[18]

The Gaps in Labor and Environmental Standards. The process of joining the disparate economies of the United States and Latin America in open trade arrangements involves problems more severe than those encountered in previous integration efforts elsewhere. Most significantly, the enormous disparity in wage levels raises the specter of unilateral relocation of industries from the high-wage to the low-wage country. This situation is compounded by other differences that define the gap between the first and third worlds—between economically advanced and less developed countries. Prominent among them are labor standards and environmental regulations. Why should it be surprising that first world and third world countries are not equal in such standards and their enforcement? No matter how intensive the negotiations, differences in labor and environmental matters cannot be bargained away. In the short term, these issues may be concealed by a cosmetic accord to make an FTA acceptable, but they may disappear only in the long term, possibly with the help of instruments like a free trade agreement.

The Infrastructure Problem. Underdeveloped countries also exhibit deficiencies in physical and human infrastructure. Gaps in wage levels, labor codes, and environmental standards may encourage firms in high-wage/high-standards economies to shift production to low-wage/low-standards partners, but inferior infrastructure deters such moves. Thus, the quantity and quality of private investment is limited by the inadequacy of roads and other transportation facilities, communications systems, water supply, electricity, worker housing and training, and other infrastructure.

If Latin American countries expect to measure the success of an FTA with the United States by the anticipated increase in private investment, the upgrading of infrastructure should be their first priority. Until this can be achieved, the United States will remain the primary attraction for investment. Not only is U.S. infrastructure superior, but the United States is also by far the largest market in any FTA. Further, by definition, firms in the United States would also have access to other markets in an FTA.

On the other hand, highly deficient infrastructure can protect high-cost domestic industry in a developing country, even if tariffs fall to zero. Transportation and other import costs may make U.S. exports uncompetitive with domestic production in the less developed country's market, a situation that is incongruous with the concept of free trade.

Firms seeking to escape high wages and/or strict enforcement of labor and environmental codes might shift production to the less developed FTA partner, but such transfers will be limited for several reasons. As indicated, underdeveloped infrastructure will be quickly exhausted if it is not upgraded. Low wages may give a firm an internationally competitive edge, but only as long as exports constitute the bulk of production and demand for unskilled labor-intensive manufacturing endures. Extremely low wages cannot generate the purchasing power to support dynamic domestic production for local markets, therefore hindering economic development. Nor can wages alone assure the maintenance of international competitiveness, as demonstrated by the East Asian countries. These newly industrializing countries have given highest priority to education and training so that the upgraded labor force will absorb higher technology for more efficient production. Rising wage levels that inevitably follow improvement in skills have not deterred the East Asians from becoming formidable international competitors.

The weak partner in an FTA must rely on confidence building to obtain the resources necessary to compete. Private funding for infrastructure improvement is rare, so funding from official agencies such as the World Bank, Inter-American Development Bank, and national governments must be tapped. This would set the stage for private investment growth sustained by a sound physical and human environment—not based on low wages or weak enforcement of labor and environmental standards.

FINAL REMARKS

In the Latin American context, unilateral trade liberalization and progress toward free markets seem to have made regional integration more viable. One might ask why Latin America would find regionalism attractive when it is already moving toward global free trade. Are regional trading blocs detrimental to the multilateral trade system, or are they the building blocks of that system? If they are building blocks, then regional integration could be a second-best solution. "If regionalism is the form that new openness in trade takes, then regionalism is more desirable than the alternative of a blocked or eroding multilateralism and is good."[19]

A convergence may develop between the "globalists" and those who view regional blocs as stepping stones to global free trade. In that function, Latin American countries must do more than reduce trade barriers among themselves, or their economic growth will be limited by regional import substitution. Their integration must be accompanied by continued multilateral trade liberalization if they want to remain on the path to international competitiveness. So far, multilateralism seems to have been more successful than economic integration in Latin America. With the advent of the EAI, the extreme asymmetry of free trade agreements with the United States may better promote Latin American integration than the more symmetrical existing subregional FTAs have done.

The United States and Latin American countries reach for hemispheric integration with similar motives. First, the emergence of regional blocs in the world economy has induced the United States to focus more attention on its own hemisphere while encouraging Latin American countries to seek safe haven through economic association with the United States. Second, recent experience has shown the United States that exports can be an important engine for economic growth, and markets in this hemisphere hold great potential. On the Latin American side, economic links with the United States provide legitimacy in the world economy, representing a country's promising economic future and worthiness of investment. Third, the U.S. and Latin American countries perceive hemispheric integration as strengthening their bargaining power with the rest of the world.[20]

Because of its asymmetry, the NAFTA is a singular experiment. The accession of other South American countries would make it even more unique. The United States and Mexico share one of the world's longest borders, and their trade ranks among the top three or four trading volumes between any two countries around the globe. No other Latin American country's trade with the United States comes close. For Mexico, therefore, the potential benefits of a free trade agreement with the United States would be much more concrete than for any other Latin American country. If symbolism plays a significant role for Mexico in entering the NAFTA, it is immensely more important for other Latin American countries.

The hemispheric experiment, absent any previous experience elsewhere, must rely on its own devices. It appears that little can be learned from the most successful integration experiment so far—the European Community—that will be useful for the EAI. Perhaps the one important lesson is that it takes tremendous financial resources to create a common market. The resources currently available and foreseen for the EAI and its hemispheric integration objective are only a tiny fraction of the EC's yearly spending.

Notes

1. Joseph Grunwald, Miguel S. Wionczek, and Martin Carnoy, *Latin American Economic Integration and U.S. Policy* (Washington, D.C.: Brookings Institution, 1972), p. 65.

2. See Arthur P. Whitaker, *The Western Hemisphere Idea: Its Rise and Decline* (Ithaca, N.Y., 1954).

3. Grunwald et al., *Latin American Economic Integration*, p. 67.

4. Albert Fishlow, "The Mature Neighbor Policy: A Proposal for a United States Economic Policy for Latin America," in Joseph Grunwald, ed., *Latin America and the World Economy* (Sage, 1978), p. 37.

5. For the Declaration of the Presidents of America and the resulting Action Program, see Grunwald et al., *Latin American Economic Integration*, Appendix D.

6. See Jean-Jacques Servan-Schreiber, *Le Défi Américain* (Paris: Editions Denoël, 1967). That book, expressing French concern about the rapid emergence of U.S. enterprises in the European Community, allegedly sold more copies in Brazil than in France.

7. Fishlow, "The Mature Neighbor Policy," p. 46.

8. Ibid., p. 40.

9. Special analyses and information on Latin American and Caribbean economic integration can be found in the issues of *integración latinoamericana*, published monthly in Buenos Aires by the Instituto para la Integración de América Latina (INTAL), an entity of the Inter-American Development Bank.

10. Current agreements provide for the establishment of a complete common market by the year 2000, with a common external tariff instituted before mid-decade. Honduras is about to reenter CACM, and recent discussions are striving to incorporate Belize and Panama into the common market.

11. In mid-1992, CARICOM members agreed to establish a monetary union with a common regional currency by the year 2000 (OAS-CECON, *TRADE NEWS*, Vol. XVII, No. 8, Washington, D.C., Aug. 1992, p. 4).

12. Translation (by the author) of Iris Mabel Laredo, "Definición y redefinición de los objectivos del proceso de integración latinoamericanas en las tres últimas décadas (1960-1990)," INTAL, *integración latinoamericana*, Vol. 16, No. 171-172 (September-October 1991), Buenos Aires, p. 10.

13. For a discussion of integration fears, see Joseph Grunwald, "Hemispheric Economic Integration? Some Reflections," in Sidney Weintraub, ed., "Free trade in the Western Hemisphere," *THE ANNALS*, American Academy of Political and Social Science, Vol. 526, March 1993.

14. See, for example, Luis Escobar Cerda, "Aspectos financieros de la integración de América Latina," *integración latinoamericana*, INTAL, Vol.17, No. 178 (May 1992), p. 55.

15. Investment diversion worries are, of course, not confined to Latin America; East Asian countries have expressed concern about losing investments to Mexico because of the NAFTA.

For a discussion of issues of investment location in a Latin American common market, see Joseph Grunwald, "Some Reflections on Latin American Industrial Integration," in José Núñez del Arco, Eduardo Margain, and Rachel Cherol, eds., *The Economic Integration Process of Latin America in the 1980s* (Washington, D.C.: Inter-American Development Bank, 1984).

16. For a theoretical discussion of the FTA expansion problem, see John McMillan, "Does Regional Integration Foster Open Trade? Economic Theory and GATT's Article XXIV," in K. Anderson and R. Blackhurst, eds., *Regional Integration and the Global Trading System* (London: Harvester Wheatsheaf, 1993).

17. Chile signed an FTA with Mexico in September 1991 that does not give the country access to the NAFTA. As of 1992, Chile is seeking either to join the NAFTA or to enter into an FTA directly with the United States.

By the end of 1991, the United States had signed 16 framework agreements (possible precursors of FTAs) covering all of Latin America and the Caribbean, with the exception of Cuba, Haiti, and Surinam. Two of the agreements were signed with regional integration pacts, MERCOSUR and CARICOM.

18. Using current rates-of-exchange conversion factors, the per capita income gap between Mexico and the United States is more than 10:1. After adjustments to approach a more realistic conversion factor (the "Atlas" method), the gap diminishes to somewhat less than 9:1. In using estimates of the respective purchasing power of the peso and the dollar (the method employed by the United Nations' "International Comparison Program" [ICP]), the difference declines to less than 4:1. No matter how calculated, the Mexico-U.S. gap in the NAFTA is still a large multiple of any gaps existing in other integration agreements. (For the latest "Atlas" and ICP per capita GDP figures, see the World Bank, *World Development Report 1992*, World Development Indicators, Tables 1 and 30, respectively, and the corresponding technical notes, Oxford University Press, 1992.)

19. John Whalley, "Regional Trade Arrangements in North America: CUSTA and NAFTA," World Bank and CEPR Conference on New Dimensions in Regional Integration, Session III, Paper No. 6 (Washington, D.C., April 2-3, 1992), p. 23. The McMillan article cited above ("Does Regional Integration Foster Open Trade?") comes to a similar conclusion, albeit under well-defined conditions.

20. In a nationally televised debate on free trade, Henry Kissinger stressed that the important U.S. rationale for the NAFTA is the enhancement of U.S. global bargaining power (Public Broadcasting System, "Firing Line," University of Mississippi, September 11, 1992).

8. The NAFTA and Developing Countries

by Sidney Weintraub

This paper addresses four themes. First, the implications of the NAFTA for Mexico, as opposed to the United States and Canada, are addressed. Second, the pertinence of the model for other developing countries is noted. Third, how the NAFTA may affect other developing countries in the areas of trade and investment diversion, potential accession of Western Hemisphere countries, and potential accession of developing countries in other regions is considered. Finally, how the NAFTA might affect the United States is discussed.

FUTURE IMPLICATIONS OF THE NAFTA FOR MEXICO

What are the macroeconomic implications of the NAFTA for Mexico? As Gustavo del Castillo V. points out, the NAFTA comes on top of an ongoing restructuring process that proceeded slowly after 1982, but which has progressed at a more accelerated pace since 1987. That restructuring process is the basis for free trade, and an open economy is the basis for Mexican growth. Accordingly, I want to give primary emphasis to how Mexico manages its own economy and will avoid giving too much weight to free trade, even though I think it is important. Free trade will matter if Mexican domestic policy is well managed, and free trade will not matter if domestic policy fails.

After many years of negative growth and severe declines in per capita income and wages, growth in Mexico began to improve around 1987. As of 1992, however, Mexican growth had slowed again. The Mexican economy grew by about 2.5 percent in 1992, still modestly positive on a per capita basis, but a full percentage point or more lower than growth in previous years. Slowing of the growth rate is the result of deliberate action—it is not an accident. Mexican authorities are concerned about the increasing current account deficit, which is expected to reach about $20 billion. That is quite substantial for a country with a gross domestic product (GDP) of only $225 billion to $250 billion. Although Mexican authorities maintain that the current account deficit is being financed, they are obviously worried, as are bankers in New York.

Another reason for the deliberate slowdown has been Mexico's anti-inflation policy. The Mexican authorities have stuck to the priority of their anti-inflation policy. The exchange rate, for example, is clearly and unambiguously being used as an anti-inflationary device. The long-term goal is to maintain very narrow variations between the market rates of the two currencies, the peso and the dollar—Mexican authorities have even talked about locking the exchange rate, although they have fortunately refrained from doing so. Keeping the exchange rates close implies convergence on inflation rates.

Mexico's policy may yet give way to more growth, especially as the 1994 presidential election approaches. In my view, Mexico is currently well poised for fairly solid growth in the future. The competitiveness of its industry is growing, the country is attracting much foreign investment, and, in addition to financing the current account deficit, Mexico has increased its reserves. In the past few years, about a third of the capital coming into Mexico has been in the form of direct investment. Political interference in the operation of the economy has decreased, and the authorities have paid attention to relative prices, not just macroeconomic elements. They are reforming the agricultural structure and taking measures that are really quite far-reaching in the context of any economy. In fact, these measures are more profound than those the U.S. has been willing to consider and, as I will discuss further, more extensive than those most other developing countries are willing to consider.

There are some clouds on the horizon. First, the exchange rate is becoming increasingly overvalued as the Mexican authorities keep the sliding of the peso to less than the differential in U.S. and Mexican inflation. Productivity has increased, but not as much as expected, and GDP growth is slower than anticipated.

The NAFTA obviously provides symbolic insurance for Mexico to obtain productive investment to serve a larger North American market. Although a lot of the investment may have occurred because of internal performance, some of it is also in anticipation of free trade and the certainty of treatment. Although there are numerous studies on how free trade will affect Mexico, they are difficult to incorporate in this discussion. One static study receiving much attention in Mexico is by an economist at the Colegio de México that shows, depending on some assumptions, about 8 to 10 percent growth in the Mexican GDP. Because it is comparative statics, the time frame in that study is flexible.

Some dynamic studies, however, show much more growth. Kehoe projects as much as 0.75 of 1 percent more growth each year than Mexico would have experienced without free trade.[1] If you compound that statistic, the outcome is quite remarkable. As a consequence of free trade, Kehoe speculates that Mexico may experience growth comparable to that of Korea. Hufbauer and Schott, making projections based on economic and historical experiences in other countries, project Mexican growth figures even higher than other static models.[2] There have also been a series of sectoral studies of Mexico. The most complete was conducted by researchers in ITAM (Instituto Technológico Autónomo de México), one of Mexico City's leading universities.

I have yet to see a rigorous study that predicts increased growth from free trade that is not based on the assumption of well managed domestic policy. This, however, is an assumption that some are hesitant to make. There is concern that growth may suffer due to the appreciation of the exchange rate. This might also affect Mexico's export situation, as the growth of exports has not kept pace with the growth of imports.

A number of studies have made predictions about the effects of the NAFTA on Mexican labor markets. I would like to address the issues of real wages and income distribution in this context.

The decline in real wages during the 1980s, from 1982 to 1987 or 1988, was close to 50 percent. It seems almost impossible that a country could suffer such an enormous decline in real wages and maintain social stability; that speaks to the general conservatism of the Mexicans.

Real wages started to grow again around 1989. The most recent decisions on Mexico's incomes policy, made at the end of 1992, have caused some uncertainty because the priority is to fight inflation, and this may result in holding down wages. It is difficult to predict whether wages will grow as much as productivity in the near future. The tremendous amount of excess labor in Mexico, coupled with a strong desire to control inflation, may keep wages down for a time.

Income distribution is another area in which Mexico lags behind its new partners in the NAFTA. Poverty in Mexico is very high. About 40 percent of the population lives below any reasonable interpretation of the poverty line. Many criticize the neoliberal model of income distribution as a "trickle down" system that favors the rich over the poor and is unable to address Mexico's serious income disparities. It may well be that the neoliberal model is undesirable in this respect, but Mexico's inequalities developed under the old interventionist model. Perpetuation of the old model in countries like Mexico and Brazil led to the most unequal distribution of wages and income we have seen in countries of their size and level of development. We should not be so quick to blame the neoliberal model for problems generated under the interventionist model. In other words, the new model cannot be much worse than the old, and it may prove to be better.

THE NAFTA AS A MODEL FOR OTHER DEVELOPING COUNTRIES

Will the NAFTA be a model for other similar North-South integration arrangements? Some similar arrangements already exist between wealthier European nations and countries like Portugal, Greece, Spain, and perhaps one day those of eastern Europe. Europe may be the only continent where such situations exist; I do not expect the less developed countries in Asia, for example, to be willing to affiliate in a similar fashion with Japan. Japan may also be less than willing to affiliate with some of the more dynamic developing countries in Asia, like Singapore and Taiwan, even if those nations want integration.

In other words, it is possible that the NAFTA will be a model, but it is unclear how closely the model will be followed. Relationships between Europe and Africa will differ from the relationship between the United States and the Caribbean or between the United States and Central America. At present, the possibility for integration of a type similar to the NAFTA depends on the state of the industrial structure in the developing country. Does it have an industry compatible with industry in the more developed nation? Are there possibilities for a good deal of intra-industry or intra-firm trade—the central components of an agreement like the NAFTA? If the developing country is essentially an exporter of raw materials, North-South integration would be relatively meaningless.

In fact, I have seen commentaries that suggest that talk of Western Hemisphere free trade may be a colonial plot to get raw materials out of developing countries. The reference is troublesome because that is not the way the world works today; that is the thinking of a past generation. Old patterns of mercantilism and colonialism have not returned in the form of regional trading blocs. Not only are those patterns morally incompatible with modern economic policy, they have also proven far more expensive than profitable for the colonial power.

I doubt whether there will be too many other examples of North-South integration. My hope is that more subregional integration occurs among developing countries. Subregional integration is happening now in Latin America at an uneven pace and in a manner different than in the 1960s. The subregional integration arrangements of the 1960s were not liberalizing agreements; they were protective agreements designed to raise import barriers and encourage import substitution. The trade policies promoted by the NAFTA and the European arrangements have no relationship to such policies. At the moment, subregional integration in Latin America gives cause for both hope and despair. MERCOSUR, by far the most important of these, is not progressing as well as it could.

FUTURE IMPLICATIONS OF THE NAFTA FOR NONMEMBER DEVELOPING COUNTRIES

The NAFTA might affect nonmember developing countries by diversion or through the possibility of accession. Most studies predict that the potential for diversion in developing countries is minimal—this is certainly true for most of Latin America. The diversion we are talking about is not about losing markets in Mexico. The developing nations of Central and South America are primarily concerned with diversion in the U.S. market. Potential diversion, particularly trade and investment diversion, exists primarily for the countries of the Caribbean and Central America that rely heavily on the U.S. market. If Mexico increases its sugar production for export to the U.S., other sugar producers of the region may suffer. If the multifiber arrangement continues, regional clothing producers may also experience diversion.

I hope that the parties to the NAFTA proceed slowly and carefully in considering the accession of other countries in or outside the hemisphere. There are two reasons for caution.

First, North America is poised to deepen if the NAFTA works. I use the term "deepen" to mean that integration must go beyond tariff elimination and investment promotion. I have in mind the need for product standards, environmental upgrading, improving workplace conditions, minimizing exchange rate fluctuations, and other variables. As deepening occurs, countries come to see that exclusion of products derives not so much from tariffs, which do not matter very much, but through all of the details like standards and regulations involved in such agreements. There are thousands of nontariff-related details that can impede trade in an integration arrangement as extensive as the NAFTA.

The scope of these activities that needs to be considered may not be as comprehensive as in the European Community (EC), but there are the critical elements of doing business in a free trade area. The United States, Canada, and Mexico must harmonize policy to the maximum extent possible, and I do not think that can happen if we include countries like Ecuador and Bolivia and even Brazil. Chile is the only country in the hemisphere that might soon be qualified to accede to the NAFTA, and even Chile's independent accession might be harmful. The necessary deepening process will be destroyed if most other developing countries in the hemisphere are admitted before it is complete.

If the less developed nations of Latin America and the Caribbean were to accede independently to the NAFTA in the near future, the agreement might be significantly weakened. For example, some Caribbean nations have suggested the option of joining the NAFTA now but instituting a long transition period. However, most of these nations would need a transition period of three or four decades before reaching the current economic standards of Mexico. The preferable approach, then, is for these countries to reach trade-liberalizing regional agreements among themselves. After achieving honest-to-goodness free trade as regional groupings, negotiating and agreeing to the basic core of a deepened NAFTA may eventually be possible for them. This is similar to what happened between the European Community and the European Free Trade Association (EFTA). Both agreements developed independently and, after a sufficient period of time, many of the EFTA countries decided to join the EC. If, in the future, other regional groupings are ready to accede under the deepening rules of the NAFTA, then their integration may be desirable.

The second reason for avoiding the quick, independent accession of other developing countries is to make sure that those countries themselves are not damaged in the long term. For most of these countries, accession in the near future would be symbolic rather than substantial. For example, Mexico has bilateral trade agreements with some of the developing nations of Central and South America. Only 6 percent of Mexico's trade, however, takes place with the rest of Latin America, and practically none of it is in industrial commodities. These agreements are basically political agreements. Now that the United States and Mexico have agreed to free trade, Mexico may have to surrender those bilateral agreements, and the political symbolism will evaporate. These countries are interested in the U.S. market, not the Mexican market, and we should help them in an honest way. Conceptual political accession to the NAFTA might hurt developing countries who would do well to form substantial commercial bonds within their own regions. It is development of these bonds that might eventually lead to substantial accession to a healthier NAFTA.

One way to avoid trade damage to other countries in the Western Hemisphere is to reach free trade agreements between the NAFTA and subregional hemispheric groupings, as the EC did with EFTA.

IMPLICATIONS OF THE NAFTA FOR THE UNITED STATES

In the short term, the effect of the NAFTA on the macroeconomy of the United States may be hardly noticeable. Some individuals, unions, and workers may be hurt, but what happens in the United States will depend mostly on Mexican growth. Since the Mexican economy began to expand after 1987, U.S. exports there have soared. With U.S. exports of over $40 billion in 1992, Mexico has become a bigger market for U.S. manufactured goods than Japan. Mexico may not be able to sustain such rapid import growth, but as Mexico grows, its propensity to import is higher than that of the United States. What happens to American exports and American jobs as a result of the NAFTA depends primarily on overall economic growth in Mexico.

Thus, those who believe that the agreement will not matter much for the United States may be reasonably correct in the short term. But if the Mexican economy grows in line with the projections I gave at the outset, so too will U.S. exports grow. All the evidence to date shows precisely that. The majority of serious quantitative studies confirm it. U.S. investment in Mexico is growing, but this does not lead to a diversion of exports. In terms of U.S. exports, intra-industry trade and intra-firm trade are expanding. As Mexico grows, it takes in most of its imports from the United States. This is less true for U.S. exports to Europe and Asia. Mexico's propensity to buy U.S. goods and services makes a big difference.

Finally, I do expect that some American workers will be hurt by the NAFTA, just as workers have been hurt by advances in technology and changes in the U.S. economy. President Clinton is correct to insist on better retraining and financial assistance packages for these Americans, and it is essential that he succeed in establishing these. But it would be a mistake to blame Mexico for all the problems that the United States has incurred because of technological and other forms of economic change. The NAFTA holds many changes in store, but these are more for the better than for the worse.

Notes

1. Timothy J. Kehoe, "Assessing the Economic Impact of North American Free Trade," *A Policy Paper on the Americas* (Washington, D.C.: CSIS, 1992).

2. G. Hufbauer and J. Schott, *North American Free Trade: Issues and Recommendations* (Washington, D.C.: Institute for International Economics, 1992).

9. Dynamic Gains from Intra-regional Trade in Latin America[1]

by Rudolf M. Buitelaar

INTRODUCTION

There are some powerful reasons to expect a significant increase in trade flows between countries in Latin America in the near future. During the past decade, the region has shown a remarkable export effort, triggered by the debt crisis. A change in development strategies and economic policies has taken shape; inward-looking industrialization regimes are passing through a stabilization phase and moving toward an export-led reactivation model of economic development. Imports were sluggish in most countries in the 1980s due to severe constraints on payment capacity. As a result, intra-regional trade was less dynamic than extra-regional trade for Latin America in the 1980s. The reactivation of the economies of the region will reverse this trend.

In this context, the Enterprise for the Americas Initiative and the NAFTA negotiations fueled an awareness among governments of the region that they should prepare their economies to compete in more open markets. A host of subregional and bilateral trade discussions between countries in Latin America are likely to increase trade in the coming years, even if the NAFTA negotiations and other trade agreements take more time than initially expected, and despite the fact that effective integration between countries in Latin America is likely to be a cumbersome process.

The debate over trade policy involves the question of whether intra-regional trade should be promoted explicitly. This paper explores some possible dynamic effects of an increase in intra-regional trade on the production structure and capacity of the region.

Arguably the most important dynamic gain of increased intra-regional trade would be an improved growth rate of the economies of the region. This argument derives from the observation that there is a strong correlation between the growth in exports of manufactures and the growth rate of gross domestic product (GDP) and from the fact that manufactures account for a bigger share of trade between less developed countries (LDCs) than for trade between LDCs and industrialized countries.

J. Arthur Lewis suggested something similar in his Nobel speech—he observed that imports of manufactures by industrialized countries are in the long run less dynamic than imports of manufactures by LDCs.

According to this line of reasoning, intra-LDC trade should therefore be stimulated in order to improve the prospects for a steadier increase in LDC manufactured exports and hence improve growth prospects. In this paper, however, we analyze other dynamic effects of regional integration that have been suggested in the literature. The older work (see, e.g., ECLAC, 1959)[2] concentrates mainly upon the acceleration of the industrialization process and the lowering of external vulnerability of the countries in Latin America. More modern work (see, e.g., ECLAC, 1990)[3] concentrates upon the stimulation of local technological capabilities—as the production of goods traded within the region is technologically more demanding than that of those traded extra-regionally—and a more solid and diversified international position for the countries of the region. These are the kind of effects this paper will investigate.

The key questions in this exploration refer to the structure and dynamics of production and trade, making a distinction between the relationships among Latin American countries and between Latin America and the outside world. First, is a development strategy that pursues intra-regional integration between developing countries different from a global export-led development strategy? The hypothesis proposes that it is part of the same strategy—that integration between Latin American countries is one part of a global opening-up strategy that pursues general export-led growth. Second, are there differences between the composition of trade flows among Latin American countries and the composition of trade flows between Latin American countries and the rest of the world?

What follows is a presentation of the data used in the research, together with a global view on the structure of production and trade and the recent transformations thereof. This is followed by two regression analyses. The first explores the relation between the intra-regional export effort, the extra-regional export effort, and external dependency. It concludes that good intra-regional performance and good extra-regional performance are compatible, as are strong intra-regional trade and an important degree of openness toward the outside world. These conclusions may help economic policymakers avoid past mistakes.

The second regression analysis explores the relation between the degree of intra-industry trade and the pattern of each trade flow. It presents convincing evidence that the degree of intra-industry trade increases with an increasing intra-regional export effort and decreases with an increasing extra-regional export effort. This finding implies that intra-regional trade has different characteristics and may be seen as complementary to the extra-regional export effort. This may spur discussion on taking positive action to stimulate regional integration.

The next section examines in detail the main product groups that have an important share in intra-regional exports. The data is presented in a two-by-two graph, establishing on the x-axis whether production is domestic market-oriented or export-oriented and on the y-axis whether trade is intra-regionally or extra-regionally oriented. It defines as "industries of regional integration" those that are export oriented and relatively more focused on the regional markets. Main sectors are chemical products, transport equipment, and nonelectrical machinery. The section examines further the competitive position of the different countries per sector.

The last section presents the main conclusions: the regional market offers opportunities to develop industrial exports that are likely to have important technological learning effects. A case can be made that regional integration should be promoted by explicit policy measures, complementary to extra-regional trade and not opposed to it, because openness of markets to third parties goes hand in hand with increased intra-regional export efforts.

PRESENTATION OF THE DATA AND SOME GLOBAL FACTS

The Data

The type of analysis proposed here requires the combination of production with trade data. The data on gross production value (GPV, also referred to as output) and employment were taken from the UNIDO Industrial Statistics Data Base at the three-digit ISIC level in national currency. The United Nations Comtrade data base provided data on trade, in current dollars, that were transformed from the SITC classification to the three-digit ISIC level through the TARS software program. The three-digit ISIC level is composed of 28 productive sectors that can be considered part of the "manufacturing industry" in a broad sense. Included here are food products, refined oil, and semimanufactures of basic minerals (normally excluded from the definition of manufacturing industry) in order to provide as ample a picture as possible of trade in goods. ISIC chapter 3 goods account for 64-77 percent of total exports of goods in the 13 countries selected for detailed analysis.

An effort was made to include every economy in Latin America and the Caribbean in the analysis. From the 25 countries with some available data, it was possible to construct a complete set of variables for only 13 for the periods 1978-80 and 1988-90. The three-year averages were calculated to improve comparability and presentation. It must be noted that data on intra-regional trade include all trade from the 13 countries within the region (the original 25 countries). These 13 countries account for around 94 percent of regional GPV, 90 percent of employment in the industries considered, and about 80 percent of regional trade.[4] The overall representative quality of these countries is therefore satisfactory.

These data present two important problems, neither of which can be solved entirely—the over- and undervaluation of national currencies and the changes in relative prices between products. The data in national currencies have been changed to current dollars using the IMF "rf" (market) exchange rate, and a correction factor has been applied to adjust for periodic overvaluation and undervaluation of currencies. This factor was calculated by estimating the trend in the Index of the Real Effective Exchange Rate (IREER, which compares national inflation with dollar inflation), and dividing the actually observed IREER with the estimated trend value. This amounts to (downward) adjustments as high as 40 percent, as in the case of Argentina for the period 1978-80.

The problem of fluctuating relative prices should be addressed by transforming the current values into constant values. This, however, could cause new problems. In this paper, distortions are somewhat lessened by maintaining the current values, concentrating the analysis in terms of relative shares and comparing the composition of production and trade. The distortions remain, however—especially due to price fluctuations in oil products—and should be kept in mind.

Some Facts about Production and Trade in Latin America

Before beginning the analysis of composed variables, it is useful to look at absolute figures of the base data. Regional exports increased considerably (80 percent in current dollar terms) between 1978-80 and 1988-90, from almost $40 billion to $72 billion. This was achieved during a period in which GPV increased 50 percent, imports increased only 20 percent (a decline in constant terms), and employment actually fell 5 percent. Another way to present the shift in orientation is through the trade balance, which went from a regional deficit of $9.5 billion in 1978-80 to a regional surplus of close to $13.5 billion in 1988-90. This was due not only to the export effort, but also, obviously, to import restrictions.

The regional picture is strongly influenced by the major economies, but the trend is similar in most countries. In 1978-80, only Brazil and Chile registered a trade surplus, joined by Argentina, Uruguay, and Venezuela in 1988-90. For Argentina and Venezuela, this is mainly explained by an absolute drop in imports. The trade surplus of Brazil is bigger than the surplus of the region as a whole, indicating that the sum of the remaining countries still has a trade deficit in the sectors under analysis.

As for the (adjusted) GPV, only Brazil and Mexico grew faster than the region's average. This implies that the share of these countries in the region's total GPV increased from 57.6 percent in 1978-80 to 74.9 percent in 1988-90, a change that occured mainly at the expense of the relative weight of Argentina and Venezuela.

Finally, the global data reveal that intra-regional trade in ISIC chapter 3 industries accounts for only 15 percent of global trade in these industries. This is due to the low share of intra-regional trade as a percentage of total trade in Mexico (7.7 percent) and Brazil (14.1 percent). In most other countries, except for Chile, Jamaica, and Venezuela, intra-regional trade is a larger share of total trade. In Guatemala, Panama, and Uruguay, intra-regional trade amounts to around 40 percent of total trade. Intra-regional trade is also a high percentage of GPV in Guatemala and Uruguay (above 10 percent), but it garners only 1 percent in Mexico and Brazil.

External dependency (imports as a percentage of apparent national consumption, ED = GPV + M – E, also referred to as demand) decreases with the size of the economy. Brazil imports only 4.6 percent of consumption, Argentina 14.7, and Mexico imports 15.9 percent. At the other end, the Central American economies have a 40 percent external dependency, and Barbados imports an exceptional 73.6 percent of consumption. The average for the rest of South America lies between 17.1 percent (Bolivia) and 34.2 percent (Chile).

RELATIONS AMONG VARIABLES

The Export Effort toward Latin America

Does a strategy of intra-regional trade fit into an overall strategy of gaining export strength in world markets and increasing openness to imports from third parties? In a cross-section analysis of the 28 sectors, export-output ratios and import-demand ratios have been calculated for intra-regional and extra-regional exports.

The hypothesis proposes that for an intra-regional export strategy to fit in an overall strategy of export-led growth and openness toward imports, a high intra-regional export effort in sector x has to be positively correlated with a high extra-regional export effort and a high import-demand ratio in sector x. Obviously, this paper does not seek to establish a causal relationship nor to "predict" the export-output ratio through the overall equation, for which a high r-squared would be required. Basically, the paper examines the sign (positive or negative) of the relationship and the statistical validity of each variable measured with the T-test.

The equation used in the first regression analysis is:

$$\begin{aligned} eola89 &= c + a(idex89) + b(eoex89), \text{ where} \\ eola89 &= X_r/GPV \\ idex89 &= M_e/(GPV + M - X) \\ eoex89 &= X_e/GPV \end{aligned}$$

$_r$ refers to intra-regional trade,
$_e$ refers to extra-regional trade,

eo = export-output ratio,
id = import-demand ratio,
ex = extra-regional trade,
la = intra-regional trade, and
89 = three-year average 1988-90.

The correlation between the export effort toward regional markets and openness to extra-regional imports is of the right sign (positive) in 12 out of 13 cases and statistically significant in 5 (95 percent confidence level) or 7 (90 percent) out of 13 cases. This means that sectors with a high export-output ratio, taking into account only intra-regional exports, overlap with sectors having a high import-demand ratio, taking into account only extra-regional imports. The correlation between the export effort toward regional markets and toward extra-regional markets is positive in 12 out of 13 cases and statistically significant in 6 (95 percent) or 7 (90 percent).

Overall, this analysis confirms the hypothesis that an intra-regional export strategy is compatible with a global export drive and with openness to third party imports. This is clearly true for the major economies of the region—Argentina, Brazil, Chile,

Ecuador, Mexico, and Venezuela—which show statistically significant results at the 90 percent confidence level both on the import-demand variable and on the extra-regional export-output ratio. Colombia is an important exception. Significant relationships are also found for Guatemala and Panama. For Barbados, Bolivia, Jamaica, and Uruguay no statistically significant correlation was found on these variables (see Table 1).

For the region as a whole, even the overall fit is satisfactory and the correlations are particularly robust.

The Degree of Intra-industry Trade

Is intra-regional trade of a different nature than extra-regional trade? The next section further elaborates on this issue, but first we will analyze the differences between intra- and extra-regional trade in the degree of intra-industry trade.*

The hypothesis underlying the regression analysis is that intra-industry trade is higher in intra-regional trade than in extra-regional trade. The equation used is:

$$g = c + a(eola) + b(eoex) + d(idla) + e(idex)$$

The regression is made for the periods 1988-90 and 1978-80. For 1988-90, the correlation between the degree of intra-industry trade and the export-output ratio regarding exports to the region is positive in 11 out of 13 cases, but only statistically significant in 3 (see Table 2). For 1978-80, the result is closer to the hypothesis: positive in 12 cases, significant in 8 (see Table 3). Perhaps the contraction of imports, which strongly affected intra-regional imports, accounts for the decrease in the statistical significance of the relationship and for the decline in the intra-industry nature of intra-regional trade. The normal situation would be similar to that of 1978-80 and would prove, though not so robustly, the initial hypothesis.

The correlation between the degree of intra-industry trade and the export-output ratio regarding exports to third parties is of the right sign (negative) in 10 out of 13 cases, and it is

---

*The traditional Grubel and Lloyd measure is used to define the degree g of intra-industry trade. The formula is: $g = (((X + M) - (X - M))/(X + M)) * 100$.

The degree g is 100 for any sector when exports are exactly equal to imports, indicating perfect intra-industry trade, and g is 0 if the sector either exports or imports exclusively, indicating absolute nonexistence of intra-industry trade.

TABLE 1

Regression Analysis of Export Effort to Latin America

		c	1	2	r^2	SE	DW	F
Argentina	c	2.01	0.06	0.12	.21	3.29	2.14	4.57
	T	(2.08)	(1.61)	(2.66)				
Barbados	c	-6.12	0.29	0.15	.09	47.6	1.71	2.38
	T	(-0.31)	(1.02)	(1.28)				
Bolivia	c	4.19	0.03	0.01	-.07	11.8	2.23	0.12
	T	(1.37)	(0.22)	(0.49)				
Brazil	c	0.56	0.10	0.03	.35	0.86	1.95	8.34
	T	(2.10)	(3.69)	(1.41)				
Chile	c	0.11	0.13	0.11	.48	5.96	1.51	13.22
	T	(0.07)	(3.03)	(2.99)				
Colombia	c	3.96	0.003	0.07	-.02	6.39	2.02	0.80
	T	(2.41)	(0.04)	(1.21)				
Ecuador	c	-0.75	0.11	0.34	.77	4.56	1.67	46.36
	T	(-0.60)	(2.90)	(9.58)				
Guatemala	c	13.09	0.15	0.05	.03	12.53	2.02	1.46
	T	(2.89)	(1.70)	(0.20)				
Jamaica	c	5.10	0.04	0.22	-.06	13.47	1.89	0.21
	T	(1.26)	(0.64)	(0.01)				
Mexico	c	-0.06	0.03	0.05	.76	0.58	1.19	44.15
	T	(-0.39)	(3.44)	(5.10)				
Panama	c	2.36	-0.004	0.30	.67	3.94	1.63	28.98
	T	(2.88)	(-1.15)	(5.76)				
Uruguay	c	13.54	0.04	-0.03	-0.04	19.21	1.26	0.49
	T	(3.24)	(0.82)	(-0.13)				
Venezuela	c	0.41	0.08	0.06	.36	2.45	1.76	8.60
	T	(0.60)	(2.96)	(3.42)				
Total Region	c	0.58	0.09	0.05	.59	0.90	1.95	20.68
	T	(1.96)	(5.25)	(2.15)				

dependent variable: eola89

independent variables:
1 = idex89
2 = eoex89

TABLE 2

Regression Analysis of the Degree of Intra-industry Trade, 1988-90

		c	1	2	3	4	r^2	SE	DW	F
Argentina	c	49.02	1.34	-1.29	6.53	-0.57	.30	23.56	2.17	3.88
	T	(6.52)	(0.82)	(-2.93)	(2.71)	(-2.15)				
Barbados	c	60.48	0.10	0.19	-0.02	-0.52	.37	22.34	1.81	5.03
	T	(5.81)	(1.11)	(3.26)	(-0.07)	(-3.89)				
Bolivia	c	24.92	0.10	-0.02	-0.48	-0.16	.05	23.17	1.55	1.35
	T	(3.37)	(0.25)	(-0.30)	(-1.60)	(-0.64)				
Brazil	c	43.30	12.75	-3.04	9.30	0.06	.47	19.86	1.22	6.87
	T	(6.52)	(2.51)	(-4.17)	(4.01)	(0.07)				
Chile	c	39.43	0.88	-0.10	0.71	-0.46	.00	24.56	2.64	1.03
	T	(5.82)	(1.06)	(-0.53)	(1.14)	(-1.98)				
Colombia	c	54.72	-0.60	-0.18	0.28	-0.73	.06	29.55	1.57	1.41
	T	(6.48)	(-0.64)	(-0.53)	(0.61)	(-2.07)				
Ecuador	c	31.43	0.57	-0.40	-0.65	-0.39	.09	22.16	2.03	1.69
	T	(4.90)	(0.58)	(-1.07)	(-0.96)	(-1.58)				
Guatemala	c	37.84	0.91	-0.24	-0.04	-0.03	.32	25.99	2.45	4.15
	T	(4.04)	(2.29)	(-0.52)	(-1.08)	(-2.93)				
Jamaica	c	34.87	0.38	0.05	-1.53	-0.04	.04	27.20	1.20	1.32
	T	(3.73)	(0.93)	(0.90)	(-1.30)	(-0.32)				
Mexico	c	59.54	0.04	-0.59	18.72	-0.32	.00	20.91	2.06	1.02
	T	(10.21)	(0.01)	(-1.21)	(1.60)	(-0.76)				
Panama	c	27.82	-0.89	1.65	-1.24	-0.05	.42	21.99	1.75	5.91
	T	(4.26)	(-0.78)	(3.77)	(-1.70)	(-2.34)				
Uruguay	c	46.77	0.19	-0.40	-0.24	0.17	.02	29.39	1.41	1.13
	T	(5.84)	(0.57)	(-1.11)	(-0.78)	(0.66)				
Venezuela	c	51.59	4.39	-0.59	1.04	-1.04	.39	19.42	1.21	5.31
	T	(8.72)	(2.68)	(-3.31)	(0.60)	(-4.16)				

dependent variable: g

independent variables:
1 = eola
2 = eoex
3 = idla
4 = idex

TABLE 3

Regression Analysis of the Degree of Intra-industry Trade, 1978-80

		c	1	2	3	4	r^2	SE	DW	F
Argentina	c	44.10	8.86	-1.72	-0.96	-1.14	.25	20	1.41	3.24
	T	(6.61)	(2.75)	(-2.16)	(-0.53)	(-2.82)				
Barbados	c	52.68	-0.07	0.27	-0.30	-0.34	.22	27.29	1.62	2.94
	T	(3.39)	(-0.70)	(3.32)	(-0.68)	(-2.05)				
Bolivia	c	29.09	0.25	-0.04	-1.27	-0.12	.14	23.65	1.57	2.06
	T	(3.80)	(0.50)	(-0.40)	(-1.49)	(-0.47)				
Brazil	c	43.80	12.38	-1.64	-1.27	-1.41	.24	25.55	1.88	3.17
	T	(4.82)	(2.65)	(-2.04)	(-0.53)	(-1.90)				
Chile	c	30.63	0.83	-0.31	0.91	-0.36	-.03	25.95	1.67	0.80
	T	(3.67)	(1.22)	(-0.99)	(0.49)	(-1.33)				
Colombia	c	37.17	3.40	-0.07	-0.12	-0.86	.21	25.93	1.54	2.80
	T	(4.03)	(2.50)	(-0.11)	(-0.14)	(-2.54)				
Ecuador	c	18.11	0.09	-0.07	-0.23	-0.24	.01	15.98	2.12	1.10
	T	(3.83)	(0.60)	(-0.95)	(-1.30)	(-1.63)				
Guatemala	c	25.40	1.04	0.01	1.37	-0.67	.61	18.01	2.45	11.71
	T	(3.24)	(3.80)	(0.45)	(2.71)	(-4.22)				
Jamaica	c	38.20	1.15	-0.08	-0.54	-0.36	.15	23.38	1.92	2.17
	T	(5.09)	(2.60)	(-1.57)	(-0.59)	(-2.06)				
Mexico	c	59.10	8.42	1.15	-2.34	-1.54	.52	18.01	2.20	8.21
	T	(12.40)	(2.17)	(1.54)	(-0.64)	(-4.23)				
Panama	c	28.98	0.35	3.84	-0.57	-0.38	.60	17.49	1.86	11.04
	T	(4.62)	(0.67)	(3.70)	(-1.45)	(-3.22)				
Uruguay	c	44.97	1.36	-0.98	-0.76	-0.61	.38	18.73	2.06	5.18
	T	(7.20)	(2.18)	(-2.31)	(-2.70)	(-2.32)				
Venezuela	c	9.47	5.69	-0.67	-0.09	-0.14	.53	13.83	1.87	8.69
	T	(1.96)	(5.18)	(-3.39)	(-0.09)	(-0.96)				

dependent variable: g

independent variables:
1 = eola
2 = eoex
3 = idla
4 = idex

statistically significant in 3 of those cases. For 1978-80, 9 cases were negatively correlated, with 4 statistically significant. Interestingly, the correlation is statistically significant but of the unexpected (positive) sign in two peculiar cases, Barbados and Panama. This might be explained by a kind of "Maquiladora" relationship, in which exports to third countries are only slightly manufactured forms of what was previously imported from the same countries. Exports from free zones are not accounted for in the data, but nevertheless the explanation might hold.

The least convincing of the four variables examined in correlation with the degree of intra-industry trade is the import-demand ratio regarding imports from the region. The correlation with the import-demand ratio regarding third party imports is much clearer. The correlation is of the right sign (negative) in 11 cases in 1988-90, and in all cases in 1978-80. It is significant in 7 (1988-90) and 9 (1978-80) cases.

This evidence, more because of the signs than because of the overall fit of the regression, strongly suggests that intra-regional trade is different from extra-regional trade. Again, this holds for the major economies of the region, with the important exception of Mexico in 1988-90 (no difference of this kind can be statistically found for this case). A singular exception is the already noted unexpected sign for Barbados and Panama.

THE CHARACTERISTICS PER SECTOR

To present and analyze the data per sector, a two-by-two graph has been constructed, with the orientation of production (orprod) on the X-axis and the orientation of trade (orcom) on the Y-axis. The formulas used are:

$$orprod = ((X_{ij}/X_j) / (GPV_{ij}/GPV_j))*100 - 100 \text{ and}$$

$$orcom = ((^{i}X_{ij}/^{i}X_j) / (^{e}X_{ij}/^{e}X_j))*100 - 100$$

The ^{i} refer to intra-regional exports,
the ^{e} refer to extra-regional exports,
the $_{i}$ refer to sector i, and
the $_{j}$ refer to country j.

If the orientation of production is negative in this formula, the sector weighs more in the production structure than it does in the export structure, and we may call it domestic market oriented. Likewise, if the value is positive, we may call it export oriented.

CHART 1
Typology of Competitive Positions

		ORIENTATION OF PRODUCTION	
		Domestic Market	Foreign Market
ORIENTATION OF TRADE	Regional Markets	"Sectors with pending reorientation" 2	"Regional integration sectors" 1
	Extra-regional Markets	"Domestic sectors with pockets of extra-regional competitiveness" 3	"International insertion sectors" 4

If the orientation of trade, the second formula, is negative, the sector weighs more in extra-regional exports than it does in intra-regional exports, and we may call it extra-regionally oriented. Likewise, if the value is positive, we may call it regional market oriented (see Chart 1).

The six sectors with the biggest share in intra-regional exports are chemical industries, food products, transport equipment, refined oil, iron and steel, and nonelectrical machinery.

Chemical Industries (ISIC 351)

This sector includes basic industrial chemicals, fertilizers and pesticides, artificial fibers, and plastics. It is a heterogeneous sector, frequently related to the presence of natural resources and economies of scale. It accounts for 15.2 percent of intra-regional exports in 1988-90 (compared to 7.0 percent in 1978-80), but only 6.8 percent of output, and 2.9 percent of employment. The sector is also characterized by a high degree of openness (it accounts for 17.1 percent of overall imports), and a high degree of intra-industry trade. This industry can be seen as a typical intra-regional trade sector.

Chart 2 shows the sector is export-oriented and focused on regional markets in seven countries (Argentina, Bolivia, Brazil, Chile, Mexico, Panama, and Uruguay), and domestic market-oriented in four (Colombia, Ecuador, Guatemala, and Venezuela). A shift can be observed toward a regional market orientation in the Andean Pact countries from 1978-80 to 1988-90. No information is available for Barbados and Jamaica.

CHART 2
Chemical Industries

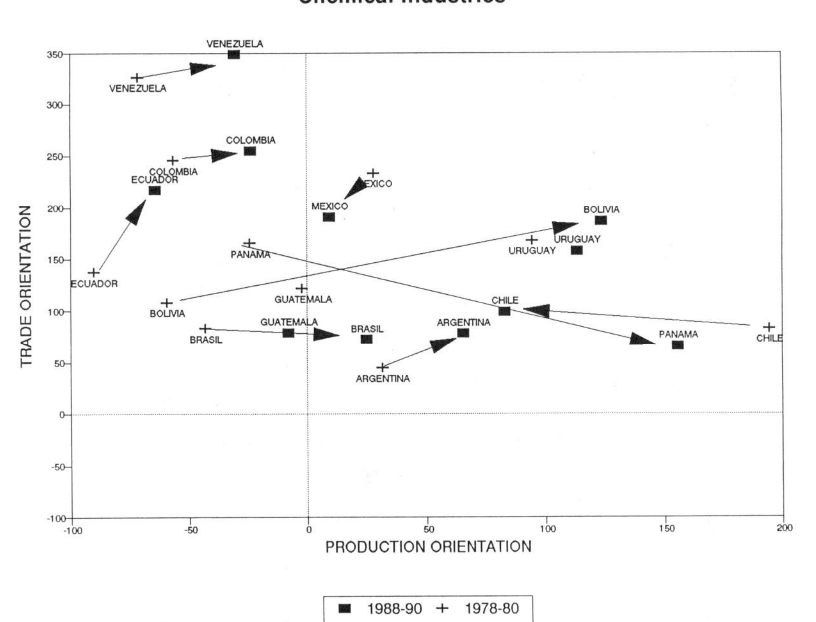

Food Products (ISIC 311-12)

The second important sector in intra-regional trade in Latin America is food products. The sector accounts for 12.4 percent of intra-regional exports, 18.2 percent of national output, and 16.2 percent of regional employment.

Chart 3 clearly shows that the export orientation of the industry is in no case dominated by regional markets. The industry is third party market export-oriented in the cases of Argentina, Brazil, Colombia, Guatemala, and Uruguay. It is a home market-oriented sector with some exports to third party markets in the cases of Barbados, Chile, Ecuador, Jamaica, and Mexico, and it is domestic market-oriented with some regional trade only in the case of Bolivia and Venezuela.

The comparison with the situation in the chemical industry is clear: in food products most countries are competitive in extra-regional markets; in chemical products they are competitive in regional markets. Both industries have a major share of intra-regional exports, but the regional market is decisive only for chemicals.

CHART 3
Food Products

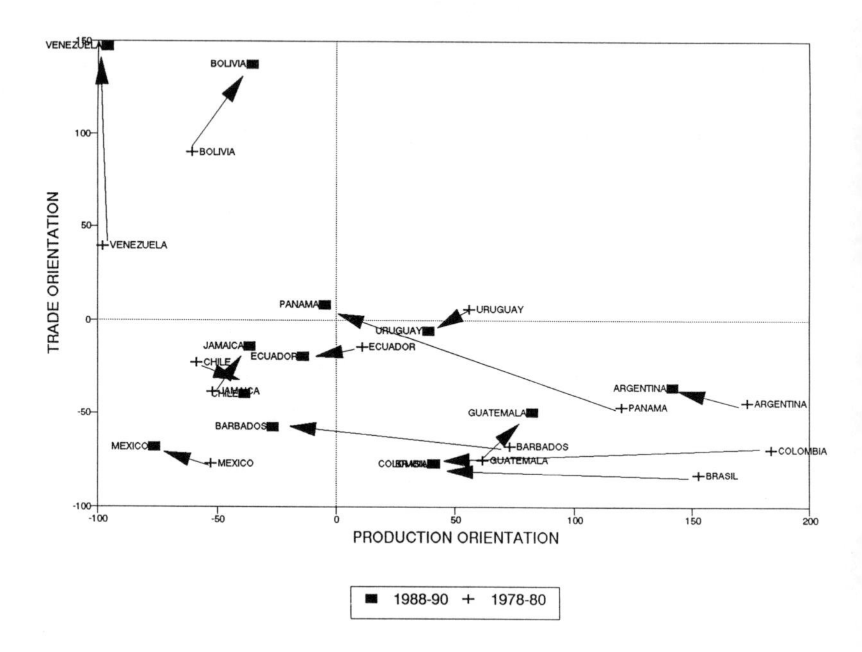

Transport Equipment (ISIC 384)

The sector third in importance to intra-regional trade includes the manufacture of automobiles, ships, railroad equipment, airplanes, bicycles, and motorcycles. The transport equipment industry accounts for 10.7 percent of intra-regional exports, showing an upward trend. The sector provides 7.1 percent of the region's output and 6.0 percent of the region's jobs.

This industry is export-oriented in only two countries: Brazil and Mexico. The difference is that Mexico increasingly exports extra-regionally, whereas Brazil exports predominantly inside the region.

Comparison with the chemical industry shows an important difference: while two countries dominate trade in transport equipment, the participation of countries in the chemical trade is more diversified. Both industries account for a large share of intra-regional exports, but intra-regional trade is vital for the sector only in the case of Brazil.

Iron and Steel (ISIC 371)

The fourth industry in intra-regional exports is the manufacture of primary products of iron and steel, from foundry to sheets of semiterminated products. The iron and steel industry has experienced a strong increase in its weight in intra-regional trade, from 3.9 percent in 1978-80 to 9.5 percent in 1988-90. It is again a relatively capital intensive industry, like others that dominate intra-regional trade, as its share of output (6.6 percent) exceeds by far its share in employment (3.4 percent). It is noteworthy, in this industry as in transport equipment, that despite an increase in its share of intra-regional exports, its share in employment has declined.

For Argentina and Colombia, this sector is export-oriented with a predominance of extra-regional markets. In the case of Brazil, as iron and steel is also an export-oriented industry, the relative importance of intra-regional and extra-regional markets is equal. This balance in destination of exports also holds in the case of Mexico, but there the orientation of the sector is mainly toward domestic markets.

This industry shows characteristics more similar to food products than to transport equipment and chemicals, as third party markets seem to be more decisive than regional markets.

Petroleum Refineries (ISIC 353)

The industry fifth in importance to intra-regional trade (8.2 percent) is refined oil. It was first in importance in 1978-80 (17.5 percent) due to price fluctuation. The countries where it is a third party market-oriented industry are the well-known oil producers: Ecuador, Venezuela, Mexico, and Colombia. The relative weight of extra-regional markets seems balanced with the weight of intra-regional trade only for Ecuador. In all other countries, it is basically a domestic market-oriented industry, in a few cases some extra-regional trade, and in others some intra-regional trade. This is clearly a branch like food products and iron and steel where third party markets are more vital than intra-regional markets.

Nonelectrical Machinery (ISIC 382)

The last sector in this analysis is comprised of the manufacture of engines and turbines, equipment for agriculture, metal and woodworking, and machinery for other industries and offices, except electrical machinery. The sector accounts for 7.8

percent of intra-regional exports, showing an important decline that corresponds with a decline in the industry's relative position in world trade.

In Argentina and Ecuador, the sector is export-oriented and focused on regional markets, although in Ecuador the overall significance of the industry is relatively low. Mexico also has an export-oriented position, and the destination of exports is equally divided between third party and regional markets. In countries like Brazil, Guatemala and Uruguay, trade in nonelectrical machinery is oriented toward regional markets, but the relative weights of its domestic sales and its exports are almost equal. Nonelectrical machinery is a relatively important sector, with a relatively high share of overall output.

Having said this, it is clear that this sector resembles industries like chemicals and transport equipment more closely than industries like food, oil, and iron and steel. The regional markets are vital for the industry in some countries. It appears similar to the chemical industry because it also offers intra-regional market opportunities for the smaller economies of the region. This sector has an openness similar to the chemical sector, as it accounts for 20 percent of overall imports, making it the first sector in this regard.

Summary of Sector Characteristics

Combined, the six major industries in intra-regional trade account for 63.8 percent of exports to regional markets. They can be divided in two groups of three: one group for which regional markets are of vital importance (chemicals, transport equipment, and nonelectrical machinery), and one group of more primary activities that, having a major share of intra-regional exports, are basically oriented toward third party markets (food products, refined oil, and iron and steel).

The three sectors in the first group also share a surprising characteristic that should not go without comment—they are precisely the industries that account for the biggest share of direct American and Japanese foreign investment.[5] The issue of the impact of foreign transnationals on intra-Latin American trade would require another study, but this indicates the importance of these enterprises.

An analysis of the position of each sector in each country clearly indicates a predominance of domestic market-oriented industries with a trade orientation to regional markets. Chart 4 summarizes this, for a total of 13 x 28 = 364 possible observations, with 20 missing observations for each period.

CHART 4
Global Results of Competitive Positions

Inward-looking regional markets: 1979: 219 cases 1989: 190 cases	Outward-looking regional markets: 1979: 45 cases 1989: 39 cases
Inward-looking extra-regional markets: 1979: 53 cases 1989: 67 cases	Outward-looking extra-regional markets: 1979: 27 cases 1989: 48 cases
Total inward looking: 1979: 272 cases 1989: 257 cases	Total outward looking: 1979: 72 cases 1989: 87 cases
Total regional market-oriented: 1979: 264 cases 1989: 229 cases	Extra-regional market-oriented: 1979: 80 cases 1989: 115 cases

The main shift is clearly from regional market-focused sectors toward extra-regional market-oriented sectors (a net shift of 25 sectors out of 344), which, as we presumed in the Introduction, might change. There was also a shift away from domestic demand to external demand, which was already clear from the basic facts presented above. Our hypothesis is that this reflects a structural change in development strategy. The most noticeable feature of Table 5, however, is the large number of sectors in which production is still basically domestic demand-oriented. This may not change very much, as it is a common feature of world economies. It is striking, however, that what trade exists in these sectors is basically oriented toward regional markets. As economic recovery in these markets gathers speed, there appears to be ample room to increase intra-regional trade.

Tables 4 and 5 present the detailed information on sectors and countries in the two situations that are most relevant to our discussion: the outward-looking sectors, both regional market oriented (Table 4), and extra-regional market oriented (Table 5).

The comparison of Tables 4 and 5 underlines a central argument of this paper: while the extra-regional trade appears to be dominated by semimanufactures and mature technologies—like foodstuffs, clothing and shoes—intra-regional trade appears to offer opportunities for a more diversified and technologically demanding group of industries—like chemicals and the sectors

TABLE 4

Regional Integration Industries

321:	Textiles	Bolivia
322:	Clothing	Colombia, Ecuador
324:	Footwear	Colombia, Guatemala
331:	Wood and wood products	Bolivia
341:	Paper	Barbados, Chile
342:	Printing and publishing	Colombia
351:	Chemical industries	Argentina, Barbados, Bolivia, Brazil, Chile, Mexico, Panama, Uruguay
352:	Other chemical industries	Barbados, Jamaica, Panama
354:	Oil derivatives	Guatemala
355:	Rubber	Panama
361:	Ceramics	Guatemala, Brazil
371:	Iron and steel	Brazil
382:	Nonelectrical machinery	Argentina, Ecuador
383:	Electrical machinery	Mexico
384:	Transport equipment	Brazil
385:	Scientific instruments	Brazil, Chile, Guatemala, Mexico, Uruguay
390:	Other manufactures	Barbados, Chile, Guatemala, Panama, Uruguay

in ISIC chapter 38. An important exception could be the relatively diversified and technologically sophisticated nature of Mexico's extra-regional trade.

CONCLUSIONS

Severe import restrictions have caused Latin American production to shift in an outward-looking direction. Intra-regional trade accounts for only a small proportion of total trade and has not been very dynamic in the 1980s, but seems to offer ample room for growth in those sectors that may face difficulties when competing in wider world markets.

The regression analyses bear out that, generally speaking and most clearly for the major economies, the export effort toward markets of the region is not incompatible with openness to imports from outside the region nor with a growing export effort to extra-regional markets. Intra-regional trade should therefore not be seen as a substitute for extra-regional trade, but as a complement to it. This would allow the diversification of the production apparatus and a technological learning process, aspects that do not appear to be present with the same strength in extra-regional trade. This thesis

TABLE 5

Industries of Extra-regional Competitiveness

Code	Industry	Countries
311-12:	Food products	Argentina, Brazil, Colombia, Guatemala, Uruguay
321:	Textiles	Barbados, Jamaica, Panama, Uruguay
322:	Clothing	Guatemala, Jamaica, Panama, Uruguay
323:	Leather	Argentina, Bolivia, Brazil, Colombia, Panama, Uruguay
324:	Footwear	Brazil, Uruguay
331:	Wood and wood products	Brazil, Chile, Ecuador, Guatemala, Panama
341:	Paper	Brazil
351:	Chemical industries	Jamaica
353:	Refined oil	Barbados, Colombia, Ecuador, Mexico, Venezuela
361:	Ceramics	Chile
371:	Iron and steel	Argentina, Colombia
372:	Nonferrous metals	Argentina, Bolivia, Brazil, Chile, Panama, Mexico, Venezuela
382:	Nonelectrical machinery	Mexico
384:	Transport equipment	Mexico
390:	Other manufactures	Bolivia, Colombia

derives mainly from the fact that intra-regional trade is more intra-industry in nature than extra-regional trade. Also, the sector analysis has identified that industries for which intra-regional trade is vital (chemicals, transport equipment, and nonelectrical machinery, among the principal ones, with scientific instruments among the more marginal ones), are technologically more demanding than those for which third country markets are vital (food products, refined oil, and iron and steel).

In some industries, a clear specialization pattern seems logical, like in the transport equipment sector where Brazil and Mexico are bound to dominate trade. These economies can be expected to hold a dominant position in most industries. Nevertheless, intra-regional trade in industries like chemicals and nonelectrical machinery seem to offer opportunities to most smaller economies as well. There is perhaps a curious contradiction here: regional markets are relatively less attractive to those countries (Brazil and Mexico) likely to enjoy the most advantages in them. For countries that might have more difficulty in the face of competition (Guatemala and Uruguay), regional markets account for a significant portion of exports. In some cases (Bolivia), even regional markets are likely to require a specialization in technologically mature industries and primary activities.

To summarize, most sectors in the first period, 1978-80, were domestic demand-oriented, with trade focusing on regional markets. Extra-regional trade was dominated by only two to four industries (foodstuffs, leather, refined oil, and nonferrous metals). Only the textile and clothing sectors exhibited the exceptional situation of being domestic demand-oriented, with trade focusing on extra-regional markets. Almost no industries were outward-oriented focusing on regional markets.

The shift of the 1980s is clear: the sectors became more outward-oriented and trade focused more on extra-regional markets. New sectors that define extra-regional trade are wood products, footwear, and to some extent iron and steel, paper, and ceramics. The exceptional characteristics of the textile and clothing markets still hold, with a less competitive position for textiles and a more competitive position for clothing. Furniture and plastics now fall in this category as well.

Of special relevance to this discussion about perspectives for intra-regional trade is the first quadrant: outward-oriented sectors focusing on regional markets. Technology-intensive industries, like chemicals, transport equipment, nonelectrical machinery, and scientific instruments, now fall in this category, from which they were previously virtually absent. For this reason, intra-regional trade can be expected to play a significant role in the technological upgrading and diversification of the Latin American production sector.

Notes

1. This paper was prepared for the International Conference of the Friedrich Ebert Foundation in cooperation with the Institute of the Americas and the National Planning Association, "A North American Free Trade Agreement: The Implications of Regionalization for Developing Countries," at the Institute of the Americas, La Jolla, California, December 13-15, 1992. For further information on data and methodology, see Rudolf Buitelaar, "Dynamic gains from intra-regional trade," ECLAC Working Paper 18 (forthcoming 1993). The Working Paper can be obtained by writing to the author, ECLAC, Casilla 179-D, Santiago de Chile.

The author wishes to thank Zaida Soto and Jaime Contador for their help in obtaining and organizing the data; Marco Dini for his advice on the design of the graphs; Graciela Moguillansky and Daniel Titelman for their advice on statistical analysis; and Juan Alberto Fuentes, Gérard Fichet and Joseph Ramos for their useful comments on earlier drafts. I accept responsibility for any errors.

2. Economic Commission for Latin America and the Caribbean, "El Mercado Común Latinoamericano," Mexico D.F., July 1959.

3. Economic Commission for Latin America and the Caribbean, "Changing Production Patterns with Social Equity," Santiago, Chile, 1990.

4. The fact that the percentage for trade is less than others may be due to the pricing problems of Cuban trade with its former allies in the Soviet bloc.

5. Interamerican Development Bank, *Economic and Social Progress in Latin America*, Report 1992, p. 232.

PART IV

MEXICAN PERSPECTIVES

10. A Critical View of a NAFTA Including Mexico

by Adolfo Aguilar Zinser

If we want to define the Mexican perspective regarding the NAFTA debate, we will have to make a distinction between the different perspectives of the Mexican negotiators. The perspective is not that of the Mexican government because the Mexican government simply has not had a unified view of the NAFTA. While some of these varied views are not necessarily expressed, there are certainly clear differences of opinion within the Mexican government regarding the negotiations and their implications.

I want to discuss a view of the NAFTA that is in contrast to that of the negotiators. Any view of the agreement is more a matter of perception than of reality because the NAFTA has not yet gone into effect. We are all merely interpreting what we believe will happen when, if, and in what form the agreement is finally implemented.

LIBERALIZING TRADE

First, we should consider those issues regarding the NAFTA that are simply not debated or challenged in Mexico. For example, there is no challenge to the notion of liberalizing trade. There are arguments about how it should be accomplished and whether one sector should be more liberalized than another. But arguments have generally supported free trade and turned away from more restricted, protected commerce. This is a crucial point to understand because, ultimately, the debate is not about free trade, but about matters associated with it. In fact, trade appears to be liberalizing regardless of what we do or fail to do with the free trade agreement.

Another issue that is really not a matter of debate is the need for and the potential advantages of signing a regional trade agreement with the United States. There is general agreement that Mexico must do this in order to build and establish conditions for future development. There are discussions, obviously, about how much emphasis should be placed on this particular regional agreement as opposed to the GATT or another regional agreement focusing on Latin America. But the different options are no longer as contradictory or exclusive as they seemed to be in the past.

POINTS OF DEBATE ABOUT THE NAFTA

So what NAFTA issues are, in fact, debated? Let us begin by discussing three things about the Mexican negotiators' positions. First, the NAFTA debate was initiated in Mexico and was guided by a sense of urgency. Above all, Mexico feared being shut out of the U.S. trade market.

Secondly, while trade is a crucial component of the agreement, the heated and contentious part is not necessarily tariff or nontariff barriers or dispute settlement mechanisms. In Mexico, the perception is that because the free trade issue is hooked to the issue of investment, what we really have is a document that provides for a comprehensive and far-reaching investment regime for Mexico. In other words, a primary objective for participating in this agreement was not increased sales of Mexican products in the U.S. market, but rather increased U.S. investment and production in our country. Since this was presented and perceived as the most immediate use for free trade, it has focused a lot of attention on the idea of a proposed free trade investment regime.

Third, free trade is tied to the issue of deregulation and the role of the state in the economy. Here the general perception is that the free trade agreement is, by itself, innocent. However, since it will incorporate parts of Mexico's previously implemented domestic economic policy into an international treaty, the NAFTA is viewed as more than what it is intended to be. There is an important perception in Mexico that free trade will chain the country to an international political instrument that will make domestic policies irreversible.

A LEAP OF FAITH

From this standpoint, the signing of the free trade agreement is perceived, and is sometimes presented by negotiators, as a leap of faith. They believe it will spark a sequence of events that will ultimately reduce the flow of migration from Mexico to the U.S. The first step in the sequence is that free trade will provide investments. Then it will provide jobs. Competitiveness is next, followed by productivity. Productivity in turn provides higher wages. Higher income levels will then help in the redistribution of wealth in the country. This will balance regional levels. This new balance will give Mexico new terms of trade internationally and in turn help level the asymmetries between the Mexican and American economies. Ultimately, of course, this will reduce the flow of migration from Mexico to the United States.

For challengers of the free trade agreement, the basic sticking point is the disparity between the Mexican and American economies. For them, any regional agreement must not only address this disparity, but be designed to eliminate it. Among other things, they believe that the agreement should be revised to provide for more active participation of the state in inducing development. There is also that side which believes that most of what will happen with the NAFTA is already occurring. So from their perspective, we are not confronted with a choice between NAFTA or no NAFTA, but rather a choice between regulating the process of integration or just letting it happen.

In addition, there are those who think that given the politics and economics of the free trade agreement, there are plenty of reasons not to want the agreement at all. Fortunately for the NAFTA, these people are becoming an increasingly insignificant part of the politically influential sector in Mexico. Most people accept the idea that Mexico must do something.

CRITIQUING THE NAFTA

From that perspective, the criticism of free trade that comes from academics, labor, and peasant leaders, nongovernmental organizations, and others is based on a set of what I call the 10 terms of redefinition.

First, there is the belief that Mexico should not enter into any trade agreement with the U.S. that is based on absolute reciprocity. Mexico should be granted special status with respect to certain key areas of the economy, such as agriculture.

The second element is the belief that regional agreements should allow a country to unilaterally exclude something from the agreement and that Mexico has not exercised with sufficient adamancy its right to exclude what it chooses. What it chooses to exclude, of course, is oil. While Mexico has managed to keep many oil questions out of the agreement, critics still perceive that it gave in by deregulating the strategic petrochemical products originally protected by the Mexican constitution.

Third, some argue that wage differentials between the two countries are the central economic motivation for the agreement. Mexico's appeal is based on its low wage rate. the NAFTA by itself is not going to correct this wage disparity unless the agreement includes provisions guaranteeing wage equalization over time.

A fourth element in the 10-point criticism of the NAFTA is the issue of employment. Many believe that the NAFTA will not create employment opportunities fast enough or distribute these opportunities equally over diverse regions. Foreign investors will direct themselves to certain geographic regions and economic sectors while avoiding other, less profitable ones. Without regulation this will create very uneven results. Therefore, the NAFTA should include provisions allowing Mexico to choose the places and sectors of the economy where it wants investment to be funneled. The assumption is that as it now stands, the NAFTA practically eliminates the authority of the government to set industrial policy.

A fifth element is the idea that the free trade agreement will form an international market between Mexico and the U.S. based on a quasi-colonial rearrangement of their markets. Unless the NAFTA provides otherwise, the kind of trade that will naturally arise between the two nations will be disadvantageous for Mexico.

The sixth concern is that Mexico's economic and social problems will only be accelerated by the NAFTA unless the agreement recognizes that exceptional steps must be taken to address social questions.

Seventh is the idea that Mexico will lose its national sovereignty by surrendering control over its own resources and by giving up the right to organize its own developmental priorities. Therefore, the agreement should set aside sufficient regulatory room and resources for the Mexican government to continue to play its leadership role.

An eighth set of objections has been raised because of the NAFTA's emphasis on foreign investment. The perception is that the NAFTA calls in foreign investors to substitute for national investors and gives foreign investment privileges over any other kind of national investment, including domestic private investment. Therefore, the NAFTA should allow the Mexican government to set a development policy for small and medium-sized domestic industries.

Ninth is the concern that foreign investors will misbehave in Mexico. Unless the NAFTA explicitly prohibits it, they will abuse the environment and exploit Mexican workers. Investors must be subject to certain codes of conduct in their operations in Mexico.

Finally, the tenth criticism is the belief that the free trade agreement will not have a decisive impact on migration one way or the other. Even if the parties were able to introduce other migration provisions into the NAFTA, migration would remain relatively unaffected because the labor market between Mexico and the U.S. is already structurally integrated. While new economic policies may affect migratory flows, the market for cheap, illegal labor will not disappear. Therefore, the NAFTA should include a chapter on the conditions under which Mexican workers may continue to enter the United States and participate in its labor market.

So these are, in general, the 10 objections. Yet there is another objection that is purely political. It is the perception in some sectors of Mexican society that the acceptance of the free trade agreement should be made conditional on Mexico's political transition toward a more democratic government. The U.S. should not sign a free trade agreement with Mexico unless Mexico has already reached certain standards of human and civic rights.

All of these objections have been bound into a few proposals for change. While these proposals do not necessarily touch upon what the free trade agreement should include, they do address what it should leave aside. In general, critics want the regulatory power of the state to be left out of the agreement.

President Clinton campaigned against trickle-down economics, which is understood in Mexico to mean that he is campaigning against neoliberal economics. If this is true, it symbolizes a recent revision of the role of the state, and Mexico should certainly not tie itself to an instrument that would completely deprive it of any regulatory powers.

FINANCING THE NAFTA

One proposal deals with financing the NAFTA. Many believe that if the U.S. signs a free trade agreement with Mexico, it must be prepared to pay for it. In other words, the U.S. should negotiate with international financial institutions to set aside a special three-country public fund earmarked for the following investments: physical and social infrastructure, education and training, health, environment, and science and technology. With financing like this, it is hoped that the NAFTA could establish norms regarding labor, safety, health, the environment, and perhaps even democratic or human rights.

What about enforcement mechanisms? All of these must be enforced by a powerful trade commission that will accept societal participation in terms of legal claims creating a legal process by which companies and individuals can be excluded from free trade privileges if they violate norms. This discussion has been going on in Mexico for months and shows no sign of abating. However, the debate surrounding these issues has not necessarily been presented in a 10-point fashion. More often, it has suffered from polarization between two radical groups. One group follows a purely neoliberal model in which everything is provided by the market and all the NAFTA must do is install itself in that market. The other believes that we must not have a free trade agreement with the U.S. because it would mean the loss of our sovereignty.

In the middle of this tug-of-war is a group who believes that we can realistically expect a good free trade agreement by insisting that our demands be included in the negotiations. The government has always argued that the free trade agreement we have now is the best free trade agreement we can get; there simply is no better option. This belief has been largely discredited by the new U.S. administration.

President Salinas has moved into the public eye and is ready to renegotiate. He has not really proposed anything, though he has thrown two ideas, compensatory financing and migration, into the ring. Also, the government is sticking to the position that it can negotiate an agreement with the U.S. regarding the environment without including standardization of norms. Since discussion of the Maastricht Treaty began in Mexico several months ago, critics have increasingly said that Mexico is getting an outdated regional agreement. Like Europe, they say, Mexico should get a state of the art treaty. Government negotiators argue that Mexico and the U.S. are forming a free trade area, not a common market. Critics argue that may be true, but it has many of the elements of the process leading toward a common market. Why not start down that path now and introduce Europe's Social Charter, its standardization of norms, or its compensatory investments?

Of course, all of this might be a purely academic discussion. While it is encouraging that President Salinas has signaled his willingness to talk about migration, a taboo subject until very recently, it is very discouraging that the government is anxious to press the agreement through Congress in the next few months. Cordoba, Salinas's Chief Advisor, told a member of President Clinton's transition team that time is everything for Mexico. While Mexico is willing to reopen the discussion about free trade, he said, the U.S. must remember that the agreement should be in place before the fall to avoid conflicting with Mexico's presidential transition politics.

11. The NAFTA: A Mexican Search for Development

by Gustavo del Castillo V.

Proselytizers never tire of telling us that the NAFTA represents a win-win situation, too good to be ignored. A free trade regime in North America undoubtedly offers options, opportunities, and institutional mechanisms superior to what exists today and what might be accomplished in a multilateral forum such as the General Agreement on Tariffs and Trade (GATT). Yet these options and opportunities are not, nor will they be, distributed equally throughout each society and between the countries involved. The three countries start from unequal positions, and the anticipated process of adjustment will be unequal. Given these inequalities, the options and opportunities presented by the NAFTA will remain asymmetrical for the nations involved.

MEXICO

It is not surprising that Mexico's major economic concerns for the past 15 years have focused on macroeconomic policy. Mexico shares a border with the wealthiest economy on earth, so it must not only expand its own economy, but it must also meet the expectations of its citizens who demand a standard of living similar to that of their northern neighbors. Meeting these standards would be a thankless job in any context, but the job is particularly difficult in Mexico. Historical experience has shown that the transformation of Mexico's different systems of production is an extremely time-consuming process. When real changes have occurred, actors from all levels of society have participated. This contrasts sharply with the method by which changes are now being sought under the guise of economic liberalization.

Mexican foreign economic policy underwent significant change during the 1980s. The changes are evident in the U.S.-Mexico Agreement on Subsidies and Countervailing Duties, Mexico's entry into the GATT, and the Framework Agreement, along with its working groups, which sought to advance sectoral trade liberalization. During this time, Mexico's commercial regime went from requiring import permits in all cases to an average import tariff of 9 percent. Clearly, trade liberalization has been the order of the day.

At the same time, Mexico has fostered an export boom. This strategy reflects the optimal direction of a transformed productive structure: the replacement of a protectionist, import-substitution model with an export-led growth model of economic development. It is in vogue to say that the import substituting industrialization (ISI) model has run its course and cannot provide the capacity for further economic growth. This may be true, but we must remember that under ISI, economic growth outpaced demographic expansion through half a century while limiting inflation to very moderate levels. This "stabilizing development" was a success, except for two factors. First, the state played an overly active interventionist role. Second, an uncompetitive industrial structure depended upon protection to maintain its markets and high prices. Accompanied by a highly pyramidal and centralized labor relations structure, there was little room for innovation. The system relied on a cozy, symbiotic relationship between the public and private sectors that encouraged rent seeking and high income inequality while providing few incentives for research and development or technological innovation.

Mexico was ready for its "great leap forward" in 1976. However, oil, old-fashioned politics, and some old politicians delayed the process another six years. This leap forward consisted of the transformation of the cartorial state, which has constrained Mexican society from colonial days to the present. In economic terms, this meant allowing production and exchange to be undertaken freely through the dismantling of a system of tariffs used to finance the inefficiency of the state.

Mexico's growth structure gives rise to two important questions. How will capital accumulation occur to further economic growth, and are the adjustment mechanisms in place to support the transition from a historically closed system to an open one? To deal with these questions, Mexican policymakers must look to "transitional economics," focusing on the short to medium term while laying the groundwork for long-range policies. In light of Mexico's integration into the global economy and multilateral and bilateral trade agreements that engage Mexican commitments, transitional economics and decisionmaking must take place within parameters that exceed national boundaries. It could even be argued that Mexico's unilateral liberalization during the past seven years was a strategic mistake in a world where concessions are made only when equivalent benefits are to be received.

The NAFTA provides an opportunity for rule making and institutionalization of a new commercial regime that allows the two weaker partners—Canada and Mexico—to gain from the effective utilization of chapters for conflict resolution through panel procedures. Yet the NAFTA has weaknesses that are directly related to its role as a developmental instrument, a role critical to industrial restructuring.

This problem is two-dimensional. First, for a decade macroeconomic conditions have severely restricted credit to Mexican entrepreneurs, inhibiting expansion and the search for new markets. Second, Mexico has been unable to formulate a macroeconomic policy of adjustment for workers and for medium and small manufacturing firms. This translates into a lack of access to new manufacturing and management technology, without which incorporation into North American or global markets is impossible. Both in Mexico and in the text of the NAFTA itself, little has been said about worker training or about the mechanisms and management necessary to handle displaced workers in changing labor markets. In fact, from the perspective of small entrepreneurs, the prospect of further Mexican trade liberalization is like looking down the barrel of a loaded gun.

These are a few of the liberalization-related problems Mexico must resolve. They are not the only ones; below is an outline of some of the macroeconomic conditions that have governed liberalization and set the parameters for trade under a North American Free Trade Agreement.

MACROECONOMIC CONDITIONS FOR FREE TRADE

It is important to note that liberalization was not just a question of removing tariffs, but also of eliminating the econo-political system that had imposed them. These changes have implied three things: redefinition of the state as a social actor; application of self-imposed and exogenously imposed limits on the intervention of the state in economic affairs; and the crafting of the necessary economic and social conditions for putting this redefinition into practice. In concrete terms, Mexico needed to control two major macroeconomic factors after 1982—inflation and the value of the peso.

From 1982 onward, Mexicans have struggled with a great paradox. A powerful, centralized state is required for a nation committed to economic liberalization to control inflation and other conditions that threaten its survival. In response to this struggle, President de la Madrid initiated an inflation-reducing measure called the Solidarity Pact.

The Solidarity Pact controlled wages, private sector prices, public goods and service prices, and the rate of currency devaluation. The Pact's relative success is due to the organic nature of the relationship between the government and Mexican labor unions. Under the Pact, inflation declined from around 125 percent in mid 1988 to around 20 percent in mid 1989. (In January 1988, inflation reached the hyper-inflationary level of 165 percent; see Figure 1.) As economic liberalization took hold, private firms increased prices. Price hikes and the elimination of subsidies drove the inflation rate to 30 percent in 1990, but it fell again to 19 percent in 1991.[1] As part of the Pact, government intervention determines the parity of the peso to the dollar. This leads to an ever-increasing trade deficit that has set the scene for further peso devaluations, either by increasing the rate at which the peso falls vis-à-vis the dollar, or by shock devaluation.

As part of Mexico's anti-inflationary policy, increasing liberalization of imports and competition have played an important role in controlling prices. Yet the greatest macroeconomic change in Mexico has been the new role envisioned for foreign investment. The Solidarity Pact constricted the Mexican economy for almost a decade; combined with fiscal efforts to control public debt, Mexico was forced to adopt an investment policy giving exogenous actors a new role in the economy. This radical departure from post-revolutionary Mexican thinking has become a cornerstone of the NAFTA.

FIGURE 1

Mexican Inflation, 1986-90

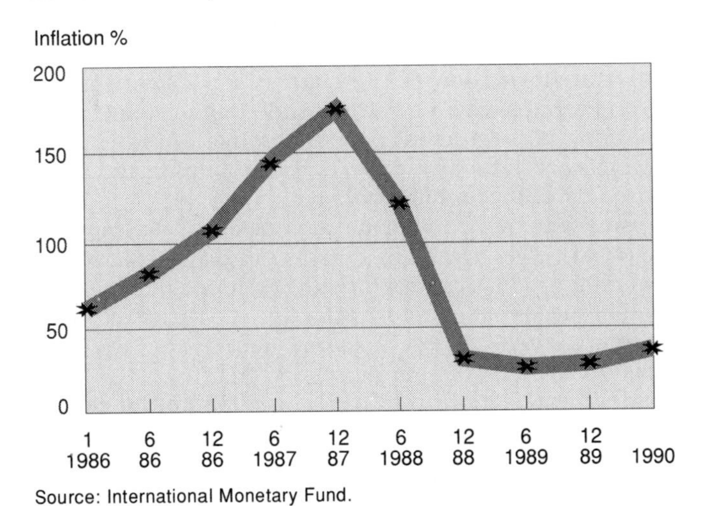

Source: International Monetary Fund.

Through much of the 1980s, economic stability was the primary goal of macroeconomic policy. The external sector played a critical role in achieving this end. In 1976, this sector was primarily composed of the International Monetary Fund (IMF) and the World Bank. In 1982, however, public sector intervention was severely restricted under the terms of the Subsidies and Countervailing Duties Agreement between Mexico and the United States, perhaps more severely than if Mexico had been a party to the GATT subsidies plan.

Another priority for the public sector in the 1980s was the renegotiation of debt with international institutions and private sector actors. Mexico had hoped that after achieving economic stability, economic growth would be possible. But while the country has experienced some of both, growth has not occurred at the government's desired rate and has been distributed unequally among different regions of the country.

Fixed investment, which increased 13 percent during 1990 and 10 percent in 1991, is expected to decrease during the next three years, dropping to 7 percent by 1995. On the other hand, foreign direct investment—which topped $3.2 billion in 1987—decreased to $2.2 billion in 1989 and increased slightly to $2.6 billion during 1990. These fluctuating investment flows are one reason why the NAFTA was necessary to guarantee national treatment for foreign investors and to strengthen protections for intellectual and patent rights. The prospect of a new investment regime under these guidelines has already attracted new investment commitments from transnationals such as Nissan, Volkswagen, Goodyear, Cummins, Hilton, and Ford Motors.[2] Mexico's endogenous capital accumulation never managed an economic transformation of the country's backward productive structure. Perhaps the new free trade regime can guarantee continued flow of investment capital, augment productive capacity, and increase jobs and exports while helping to cement decade-old neoliberal economic policies.

These economic transformations designed to improve Mexican society are constrained by holdovers from the old society and by recent changes in Mexico's foreign economic policy. Two of the primary macroeconomic factors affecting the future of the NAFTA are the increasing current account deficit and the resulting pressures on the peso.

Trade liberalization from the late 1980s to the early 1990s explains a large portion of the current account deficit (see Figure 2); much of this deficit reached nearly $3 billion, mostly through the import of intermediate goods. In response to this problem, the public sector decreased its imports 6 percent during 1991,[3]

FIGURE 2

Mexican Foreign Trade (Exports & Imports), 1980-90

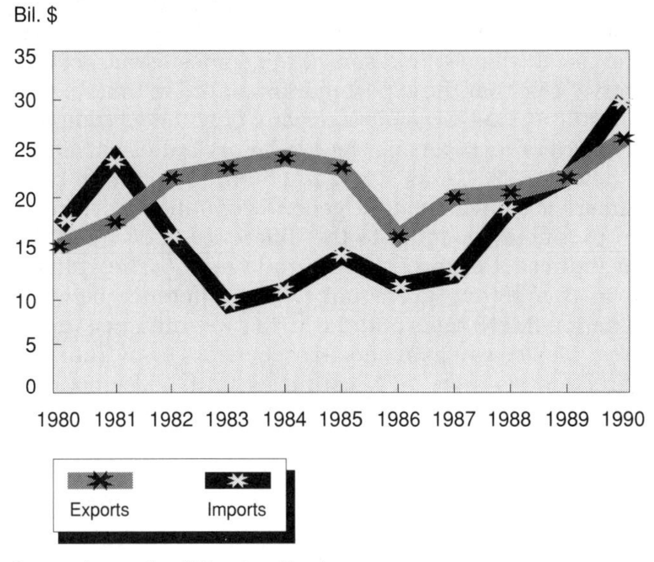

Source: International Monetary Fund.

and by March 1992, the current account deficit reached $5 billion.[4] The growing current account deficit could have been predicted, and not solely because of liberalization. The growing Mexican economy required imports for development, which translated into Mexican exports that offset the deficit. Unfortunately, the current recession in North America has reduced the demand for Mexican exports, and new foreign investment has not met Mexican expectations, giving Mexico little capital to finance this deficit.[5]

In spring 1991, while preparing for the fast-track debate in Washington, Mexican trade negotiators argued that the current account deficit would be self-financing. However, they never explicitly stated that foreign capital was to play the key role and that further liberalization measures might depend on the flow of this strategic resource.[6] The end result came in November 1992, when Mexico increased tariffs on the two products with the greatest import growth: pork and beef. These increases do not signal a withdrawal from past liberalizing policies, but they do indicate that liberalization not resulting in adequate economic growth is a flawed strategy.

Perhaps the NAFTA is a bit of smoke and mirrors. It shifts our anticipation of economic growth to Mexico's external sector while allowing the internal market to remain constricted through wage and fiscal policies. In a sense, the domestic market is playing the "reserve" role that the export market played in times past. Today the domestic market becomes relevant only when companies encounter barriers to exporting. As I have argued elsewhere, Mexico should view the NAFTA as a way to obtain preferential benefits in North America equivalent to a generalized (and false) increase in Mexican productivity, equal to the difference between MFN duties and the reduced tariffs of a free trade area.[7] The gains Mexico obtains in this setting are equal to the difference between most favored nation (MFN) rates and the tariff rates obtained under a free trade area. Mexico can gain short-run benefits from trade diversion in its direction vis-à-vis MFN countries until these countries improve their long-term productivity, offsetting any free trade gains made by Mexico. As the NAFTA stands today, the 15-year phase-in period can be seen as a grace period for Mexico to obtain real, wide-ranging productivity gains without falling behind developing countries with MFN status.[8]

SMALL AND MEDIUM-SIZED MANUFACTURING FIRMS: THE PRODUCTIVE BASE FOR DEVELOPMENT IN NORTH AMERICA

The principal issue in this discussion is the role that the NAFTA can play in Mexican development. Therefore, the rest of this paper is devoted to the results of a 1989-91 survey of small and medium-sized manufacturing firms in Canada, Mexico, and the United States, investigating the relationship between the internal conditions of these firms and their attitudes toward free trade in North America. Although the survey covers all three countries, my comments focus on Mexican enterprises, with some comparisons when necessary.

The focus on small and medium-sized enterprises arises out of the belief that they will be key agents in the new North America. These firms are essential actors in the Mexican economy just as they are in the U.S. and Canada. It is important to link macroeconomic policies in Mexico to the perspectives for economic growth possessed by these firms, because their perceptions of current macroeconomic conditions dictate how they might operate under the NAFTA. Through major adjustments, they could

TABLE 1

Firms' Opinions on Free Trade as a Mechanism to Obtain Competitiveness, 1990

	Trade with the United States	Global Trade
In agreement	76.1%	68.4%
In disagreement	4.3	19.6

Source: Gustavo del Castillo V., *Tripartite Survey of Firms, 1990* (El Colegio de la Frontera Norte/Carleton University, Ottawa/International Development Research Centre, Ottawa).

become active players in the North American economy, or they could become extinct. Another reason for focusing on these industries ties into the concept of economic democracy. These small and medium-sized enterprises may have the capacity to serve as the basis for a redistribution of wealth in Mexico under a restructured economy.

The Mexican Case

One year before the official Mexican announcement that free trade talks would begin in 1991, small and medium-sized manufacturing firms in Mexico were enthusiastic about trade liberalization with the United States (see Table 1).[9] However, many of the firms said they would need to entirely restructure their organizations to compete in the North American or world markets. This transformation would be necessary in order to alter the firms' traditional orientation toward the internal market. The

TABLE 2

Firms' Opinions on Forms of Protection Under Free Trade, 1990

	Assistance for Workers	Contingency Protection
In agreement	56.5%	66.4%
No opinion	20.7	9.8
In disagreement	19.6	20.7

Source: Same as Table 1.

TABLE 3

Types of Services Firms Need Most, 1990

Financial services	40.2%
Communication services	14.1
Computational services	28.3
No answer	15.2
Others	2.2

Source: Same as Table 1.

firms also expressed a reservation about Mexican economic liberalization that stemmed from Mexico's joining the GATT and other liberalizing policies of the 1980s: 57.6 percent of the firms believed that the process of liberalization was too rapid and that some forms of protection should remain. Support was high for programs such as worker assistance and contingency protection (see Table 2).

Of the firms surveyed, 70.7 percent thought that most Mexican firms still needed some type of protection. Yet a surprising 63.0 percent stated that it is not the government's responsibility to intervene through foreign economic policy in favor of Mexican industry. Close to 20 percent of all firms said the appropriate role of government is only supervisory. The survey also found a high correlation between the opinion that Mexico's economic liberalization has been too rapid and the belief that industry still needs a high degree of protection (r = .45). It is interesting to note that the belief that liberalization has been too rapid correlates most significantly not with support for workers' protection (r = .27), but with support for contingency protection for firms (r = .45).[10]

It is not surprising that firms should favor trade liberalization and trade protection at the same time. To be able to export with few obstacles while restricting competition at home is the best of both worlds. Small and medium-sized Mexican firms are, in effect, seeking this ideal world. They want protection at home because 86 percent of the industries have sales concentrated in the domestic market, and the existing macroeconomic conditions make them uncompetitive in North American and world markets.

When asked which services these industries would most likely need to cope with economic liberalization, they identified financial services, computational services, and communication services, in that order (see Table 3).

TABLE 4

The Human and Capital Resource Mix Firms Seek to Obtain Competitiveness, 1990

Type of worker most desirable to hire	Professionals	28.3%
	Highly trained technicians	45.7
	Medium trained	7.6
	Others	2.2
	No answer	16.3
Preferred uses of capital	Advanced technology	62.0
	Medium technology	31.5
	Others	1.1
	No answer	5.4

Source: Same as Table 1.

These industries appear convinced that competitiveness lies in increased technological knowledge, and they seek access to human and capital resources to meet this need (see Table 4).

This combination of human and capital resources has several implications for public policy in Mexico. First, it requires an industrial policy that emphasizes educational and technical achievement, and the development of the programs necessary to link industry with technical centers. Second, it mandates a monetary policy that frees and accounts for the capital needs of these kinds of enterprises.

Nevertheless, macroeconomic adjustments to meet the competitive challenge of open markets are of little use when we

TABLE 5

Firms' Conditions for Obtaining Global Competitiveness, 1990

Needs:	
1. Specialized personnel with knowledge of world markets	15.2%
2. Joint ventures	2.2
3. Partnerships with foreign brokers	15.2
4. Internal reorganization of firm	26.1
5. Additional capital	31.5

Source: Same as Table 1.

consider the internal conditions of these firms. The conditions for gaining competitiveness at a global level are shown in Table 5.

Besides their extreme need for capital investment, many of these enterprises feel that competitiveness will come only with internal reorganization. As noted above, many said they would need to entirely restructure to compete in North American or world markets. Thus, their expressed need for technical personnel (Table 4) can be interpreted as a need to fill productive and managerial functions and as a need for personnel, either in-house or foreign, with knowledge of the intricacies of international trade. This need for information explains the inability of 15.2 percent of the firms to identify the services they need most (Table 3) and the failure of 16.3 percent of the firms to identify the type of workers they should hire (Table 4). In summary, given this knowledge-managerial gap, the firms place their hopes on technology as the means to competitiveness.

These organizations' plans for further economic liberalization and integration are characterized by a high degree of flexibility. This pragmatism differs substantially from the old Latin American Common Market, in which policies and processes were set in stone and integration proceeded minute-step by minute-step. The question, then, is how the NAFTA might change this flexibility and pragmatism. The danger is that the set of rules established under the NAFTA might create new macroeconomic conditions that restrict the flexibility these firms feel is required to accomplish integration.

MACROECONOMIC CONDITIONS AND LATIN AMERICA

With few exceptions, the liberalizing policies adopted by Mexico over the past 10 years have spread to much of Latin America. There are increasing and renewed efforts at regional integration, such as the Grupo de los Tres (which includes Mexico, Colombia, and Venezuela); MERCOSUR (which includes Argentina, Brazil, and Uruguay); the Central American association with Mexico under a free trade regime effective 1996; and the Mercado Comun Centroamericano (MCCA). These efforts demand, at the very least, similar macroeconomic policies in all countries involved to ensure a level playing field for integration. These new efforts at integration seem highly pragmatic, leading to ad hoc measures instead of the detailed yet unaccomplished plans of previous efforts such as the Latin American Common Market. For example, the Action Plan of the Pacto Andino states that member countries will "dispense with formal prerequisites which characterize orthodox integration schemes."[11] Further, in

TABLE 6

Intra-regional Exports as a Proportion of Total Country Exports (FOB %)

Country	1988	1989	1990
Brazil	11.9%	11.2%	12.0%
Chile	13.5	11.2	12.6
Mexico	7.2	6.6	4.8
Venezuela	9.7	12.3	7.3

Source: Eduardo Ortiz, "El Grupo de los Tres: Una aproximación económica," in Fundación Friedrich Ebert de Colombia (FESCOL), *El Grupo de los Tres. Políticas de Integración* (Bogotá, Colombia: FESCOL, 1992), p. 103.

the documents signed in July 1986, MERCOSUR adopted a four-point strategy emphasizing flexibility:

> (i) integration would be gradual, with clearly defined phase-in periods suitable for evaluation; (ii) flexibility would be obtained through flexible rates of change and with the option to modify objectives; (iii) each phase-in period should have limited but wholly integrated objectives. To obtain this integration it would be possible to call on the harmonization of national policies; (iv) integration must demonstrate symmetry in its effects, guaranteeing that no one economy becomes specialized in any one area.[12]

This new flexible approach to integration should be welcome in Latin America—a common regional destiny that was a keystone of Simon Bolivar's vision for Latin America. Despite this flexibility, the NAFTA imposes some new parameters on the foreign

TABLE 7

Intra-regional Imports as a Proportion of Total Country Imports (FOB %)

Country	1988	1989	1990
Brazil	10.9%	15.2%	15.3%
Mexico	2.1	2.6	3.0
Venezuela	11.2	12.2	12.4

Source: Ortiz, "El Grupo de los Tres," p. 104.

economic policy of Latin American countries. Among the most serious is the reinforcement of Mexico's trade with its northern neighbors and not with Latin America. In fact, Mexico's trading relationship with the countries of Latin America seems to be declining (see Tables 6 and 7), with intraregional Mexican imports following more or less the same tendency.

The unidirectional nature of the NAFTA trade is reinforced by rules of origin that many claim are exclusionary and violate Article XXIV of the GATT. Also, with the NAFTA in place, Mexico will become a major source of trade diversion, negatively affecting Latin American trade with the United States. That is, Mexico can manufacture and export most of the goods produced by other Latin American countries, affecting not only their international trade but also their hopes and expectations for further regional integration efforts.

If the NAFTA is to be used as a model for Latin America's articulation with the United States, the region's governments have to guide public policy within boundaries they might not have contemplated. Mexican foreign economic policy is viewed as an example for the rest of Latin America, and it is difficult to say whether the internal or external conditions that determined Mexico's direction can be duplicated in other countries of the region. The flexibility contemplated in the differing integration arrangements throughout the continent may suffer a setback if the NAFTA rules are generalized regionally.

If Mexico's participation in the NAFTA provokes massive trade diversion, there are three ways that other Latin American countries can avoid the deleterious effects of such action and still participate in North American markets. First, they could invest in Mexico to meet the rules of origin problem for further exportation to North America. Second, they could sign additional free trade agreements with Mexico, thus reversing the decline in intra-regional trade. Finally, they could make use of the still-ambiguous incorporation clause of the NAFTA. Which of these three strategies (or combination of them) Latin America will choose to implement is still unclear. What is clear is that if none is implemented, the neoliberal model of trade liberalization now in place in Latin America will be in danger, and the region's hope for an increased standard of living will vanish.

Notes

1. During an address to businessmen at El Colegio de la Frontera Norte, Tijuana, B.C., on November 18, 1992, President Salinas announced that inflation during 1992 would be controlled at 11 percent. He further said

that annual inflation during 1993 would be held to 9 percent, the first time that inflation would be in the single digits in a generation.

2. The relationship between the current export boom in Mexico and the role that transnational companies are playing has been analyzed by a number of Mexican authors. See for instance: Celso Garrido, "El nuevo patron privatista, transnacionalizante y exportador para la acumulación de capital en México," in *Revista de Ciencias Sociales*, Universidad Autónoma Metropolitana-Atzcapotzalco, (Mexico City, 9:28, October-December 1989). See also Kurt Unger and Luz Consuelo Saldaña, "Las economías de escala y de alcance en las exportaciones mexicanas más dinámicas," in *Trimestre Económico* (Vol. LVI), Mexico City, April-June, 1989. These analyses emphasize the concentration of exports in a few industries and the intra-industry nature of these exports.

3. Banco de México, *Mexico in Figures* (September 1991), p. 379.

4. Banco Nacional de México, *Review of the Economic Situation of Mexico* (Vol. LXVIII, No. 803), October 1992, p. 525.

5. One outstanding characteristic of what is described as foreign investment is a tendency to be speculative and short term, going primarily to Mexico's stock market. Productive foreign direct investment (FDI) does not meet Mexican needs, while repatriation capital seems to be directed toward maintaining existing productive structures and not toward creating new industries.

6. Author's interviews, Washington, D.C., January-June 1991.

7. Gustavo del Castillo V., "La política de libre comercio y la falta de opciones mexicanas," in Fundación Friedrich Ebert, *El Grupo de los Tres* (Bogotá, Colombia, 1992).

8. When comparing the experience of countries like Spain, Portugal, and Greece in the European Community, much has been said about the decisive role that structural funds have played in their adjustment to the developed environment of western Europe. It is clear from the NAFTA process that similar adjustment funds have never been contemplated, yet it would be interesting to argue that the preferential treatment of a developing country like Mexico is somewhat equivalent to transferences from the richer to the poorer nation. Nevertheless, unlike EC structural funds, these North American transferences go not to the poorer regions or sectors of the economy, but to the well-established exporters. This exacerbates the conditions of inequality that structural funds were created to diminish.

9. Many of these research results have been published previously. See Gustavo del Castillo V., "El tratado de libre comercio y las empresas manufactureras mexicanas," in *Comercio Exterior*, Vol. 41, No. 7, July 1991. Also see del Castillo and Gustavo Vega Cánovas, "Perspectivas sobre el libre comercio: un estudio comparado de empresas mexicanas y canadienses," in *Frontera Norte* (El Colegio de la Frontera Norte, Tijuana, Vol. 3, No. 6), July-December 1991.

10. All Pearson correlations reported are significant either at the .01 or .001 level.

11. See Germánica Salgado, "La crisis de la integración," in Victor L. Urquidi and Gustavo Vega C., *Una y otras integraciones* (El Colegio de México/Fondo de Cultura Económica, Mexico, 1991), p. 196.

12. Luis Carlos Costa Rego, "La experiencia del Brasil en los distintos esquemas de integración económica Latinoamericana," in Urquidi and Vega C., *Unas y otras integraciones*, p. 276.

12. Mexican Economic Development and the NAFTA

by Daniel Szabo

In looking at the development impact of the NAFTA, we must examine the agreement in the context of both old and new development models adopted by Latin Americans in the past few years. The inward-looking development strategies and the import substitution pursued in Latin America from the 1950s until the 1980s had mixed results. While significant economic growth rates, creation of an industrial base, achievement of high nutritional standards, increased adult literacy rates and reduced infant and child mortality occurred at first, the region continued to suffer from poor income distribution, poverty, and vast inequality.

GROWTH AND EQUALITY

The competing goals of growth and equality were never adequately solved by these models. Periodic outbursts of populism emphasized redistribution at the expense of growth, often delaying development while making poverty more widespread. Although these strategies encouraged the development of industry, new industrial enterprises were never really competitive in the world market.

The subregional integration movements of this period were designed to insulate member countries from outside economic forces, thereby creating a hothouse atmosphere for domestic economics. However, state intervention not only failed to produce expected economic benefits, but it also placed greater strain on national budgets. The Latin American debt crisis of the 1980s, caused by both external and internal factors, and massive capital outflows dealt the final blow to this insulated model.

Since the mid-1980s, Latin American countries have largely abandoned an inward-looking model in favor of market-oriented economic strategies, trade liberalization, and a return to democratic processes. The latter is particularly important because a democratic framework may provide a more favorable atmosphere for the resolution of conflicting goals of growth and inequality.

We have also seen a revival of subregional economic integration strategies. By joining together, Latin Americans hope to compete more effectively in international markets. The region's declining share of world trade has not gone unnoticed. Since 1950, for example, Latin America's share of world trade has fallen from approximately 10 percent to less than 4 percent.

Mexico is, of course, one of the countries that adopted these new market-oriented strategies. It opened its markets, implemented sweeping economic reforms, and joined the GATT in 1986. These changes have already yielded significant benefits, and the NAFTA is part of the reform strategy Mexico began in the mid-1980s. Through the NAFTA, Mexico hopes to ensure access to its most important markets and convince investors that its economic situation is not only favorable to them, but long-lasting as well. By promoting its economy, the Mexican government hopes to provide increased income and a high standard of living for its people.

MEXICAN ECONOMIC AND SOCIAL DEVELOPMENT AND THE NAFTA

As part of Mexico's new development model, will the NAFTA promote both economic and social development in Mexico? Although I do not believe that the NAFTA can independently solve Mexico's development problems, the agreement should provide significant benefits for the country. Most studies indicate that the potential rewards (including new jobs, increased agricultural and industrial production, higher employment, and better wages) will outweigh the costs involved.

Will the NAFTA generate social benefits or costs? Because the NAFTA will create a free trade area and not a common market or a customs union, it lacks some of the dimensions of the European Community. Although it provides for a Trade Commission and Secretariat, the NAFTA will not provide for common development financial institutions, coordinated economic and social policies, or truly powerful supranational governing bodies. Does this mean the NAFTA will never have a social development fund or common financial institution? I think the creation of such a fund is improbable, though certainly not impossible. From the U.S. side, the NAFTA began as a commercial agreement; the social dimension was never its focus. Recently, due to emerging political forces in the United States, labor and environmental issues have become more important. In addition, President Salinas has also raised the issue of a development fund. However, it is questionable whether any of this will amount to more than a few minor changes to calm groups concerned with environmental and labor issues. I simply do not see a social fund for Mexican workers being created from U.S. funds.

THE ADVANTAGES OF THE NAFTA

Will the NAFTA do more for Mexico or more for Canada and the United States? The information I have seen points to Mexico as the principal beneficiary. Canada will gain largely by avoiding discrimination in a Mexican market. The United States, of course, will obtain many advantages. The U.S. will have better market access for many of its goods and will obtain better protection for intellectual property rights. American industries will be able to move to Mexico and take advantage of lower production costs, while increased Mexican growth rates will create new export opportunities for U.S. high technology firms in Mexico.

However, because the economies of the United States and Canada are much larger than Mexico's, I believe that the NAFTA's overall impact on the U.S. will probably not be as significant as many critics and supporters believe. We all know that an economy is constantly in the process of transformation—noncompetitive sectors decline and competitive sectors expand. Some of this is due to domestic competition between firms and some of it is due to international competition. Sooner or later, however, with or without the NAFTA or other forms of trade liberalization, noncompetitive sectors will either decline or become more competitive. In this sense, the NAFTA provides a unique opportunity to facilitate the process of transformation in the U.S., Mexico, and Canada.

THE SOCIAL IMPLICATIONS OF THE NAFTA

I must emphasize, however, that while the NAFTA will not have an enormous impact in an economic sense, it is tremendously important in a symbolic and political sense. Economically, it began with and continues to have a limited scope. But if Latin American governments view the NAFTA as the "new" U.S. policy toward the region, then development of the NAFTA's social dimension becomes even more important.

In conclusion, I believe that Latin American countries will have little choice but to continue pursuing the essential elements of their current stabilizing macroeconomic policies. Now that President Bush is out of office, there is a temptation on behalf of some Latin American leaders to reject neoliberal economic policies and begin again. I do not believe, however, that going back is an option. What is needed in the case of the NAFTA in particular and Latin American reform in general is a much greater emphasis on the social sector. Latin America needs better strategies for development and increased spending on programs such as health, technology, education, and worker training.

If the 1990s are to be the "development decade," the social dimension will have to be given higher priority by Latin American countries and by the international financial institutions supporting them.

13. Mexico's Interests and the NAFTA

by Jorge Bustamante

A Mexican saying claims that politics is the art of doing what is possible. The balance of power between Mexico and the United States is asymmetrical, and from a political perspective, it seems possible that Mexico can correct this imbalance by decree. The asymmetry is very dynamic, however, and political and economic conditions in the different regions within the two countries play increasingly important roles in the U.S.-Mexican relationship. We are no longer able to speak about Mexico as a homogeneous entity and to make generalizations about economic development without identifying distinctions between different regions and different sectors of the economy.

When examining Mexico, an underlying assumption should be that it is a nation of enormous contrasts. Certain developments have allowed the industrial sector of the country to compete with some of the most advanced in other parts of the world. At the same time, other sectors resemble some of the poorest, most underdeveloped countries of the world. This contrast must be taken into account in order to understand what is occurring in Mexico regarding the NAFTA. A generalization leaning toward one extreme or the other is going to be problematic, if not mistaken.

In this context, this article discusses the question of international labor migration from Mexico to the United States, beginning with some basic assumptions. First, the NAFTA originated a political strategy that was the best option in the absence of other feasible options for Mexican economic development. Economic development was primarily a strategy to create a massive number of permanent jobs, under the assumption that the creation of these industrial jobs would improve income distribution in Mexico. This is an important facet of economic development because, within the Western Hemisphere, income inequality in Mexico is second only to Brazil. It was assumed that an improvement in income distribution would in turn improve the standard of living of the Mexican people. Obviously, this logic cannot be applied in a homogeneous way to all conditions in all regions of the country. It applies only to certain conditions, understanding that the Mexican people must be able to benefit from the opportunities conceptualized in the free trade agreement.

President Salinas originally proposed the NAFTA. This is a fact that must be emphasized to combat the negative impression that the NAFTA is somehow a result of the asymmetry of power between Mexico and the United States or an imposition of the United States upon the less powerful nation of Mexico. It is important to clarify the position of the President of Mexico vis-à-vis the President of the United States. Critics have asserted that President Salinas somehow put all of his eggs in one basket by dealing with President Bush, when in reality he had no choice. The Mexican government, represented by the head of state, dealt with the U.S. government, represented by the head of state, and negotiations began. In fact, the NAFTA took the U.S. government by surprise. In Mexico, however, free trade was an option that was carefully studied prior to any public proposition; it was conceptualized in the context of a very difficult process of negotiation.

THE NEGOTIATING PROCESS

One of the difficulties surrounding the social dimension of free trade arose very early in the negotiating process. In fact, before the formal process of negotiations started, the U.S. government established one very clear basic premise—labor migration was not on the negotiating agenda. Again, if politics is the art of what is possible, then Mexico had two options. The Mexican negotiators could insist on a political dimension to cover the social preoccupations of many people in Mexico, or they could insist on the risky option of trade liberalization. In that situation, the social dimension possibilities relating to labor questions were completely cut from the context of negotiations.

Political and economic conditions changed greatly during the two years of negotiations. From the beginning, the Mexican government decided to open the process of consultation to representatives of different sectors of the economy. They organized the advisory committee on the free trade agreement negotiations, consisting of representatives of the business, organized labor, agricultural, and academic sectors of Mexican society.

It could be argued that this is not a completely accurate representation of all parts of the Mexican economy. Many groups, however, spoke openly in favor of their own interests, demonstrating tremendous disagreement among the different sectors. Regardless of what happens with the NAFTA, this debate spurred tremendous progress in the organization of the business community in Mexico. Organization of the private sector had no historical precedent; never before had such diverse segments of the

Mexican economy united in such an effort. This new network, connected through state-of-the-art communications technology, became involved in the creation of the "next-room" negotiating context. Private sector representatives were always in the next room with the negotiators, making sure that whatever was negotiated had their backing.

To say that these negotiations were conducted in secrecy, without the knowledge of the Mexican people, is simply not true. Obviously, however, an essential element of any negotiating process is that the various sides do not show all of their cards to the public. Negotiations proceed through a mechanism that has been agreed upon by those involved, not through the mass media, political parties, or other institution. In this way, each country is assured that its best interests are being advanced.

The negotiations were in some ways a reflection of the asymmetry of power between Mexico and the United States. Canada played a balancing role, sometimes leaning to one country, sometimes to the other. During these negotiations, there was a certain understanding that the question of asymmetry had to be dealt with in terms of the gradual implementation of the agreement. Although this was an explicit way to address the asymmetry, it may not have been sufficient. The President of Mexico has signed the treaty, but this was just a bureaucratic way of allowing the executive and the legislative branches of the other two countries to settle the details still in dispute.

NEW QUESTIONS FOR FURTHER NEGOTIATION

For Mexico, the results of the November election in the United States created a different dimension that must be negotiated. There are no formal negotiations remaining over the draft that has already been finalized, but when the results of the elections were known, Mexico and the United States entered a new political context in which negotiations had to resume. A number of channels functioning simultaneously resulted in a multitude of different communication efforts. It would be simple-minded to think that the Mexican government would now use only one channel after establishing a negotiating process in which the business communities of all three countries were actively involved.

The political agenda of President Salinas aside, an economic strategy has been discussed, supported by the private sector, and introduced to organized labor and agriculture. These groups have all presented their cases, and the resulting agreement was finalized with a great deal of national consensus. More than 80 percent of those polled are in favor of the free trade agreement negotiated by the Mexican government.

Since the November elections in the U.S., however, a different field has opened. Informal negotiations are taking place, and that is the context in which the recent statements made by President Salinas must be understood. If details in the areas of labor or environmental regulation have been placed back on the bargaining table, the present agreement may change, but not without cost.

In terms of environmental issues, there is little disagreement; the two sides share basically the same definitions at the government and grass-roots level, and neither country wants to do anything that will hurt the environment. Some in the United States mistakenly believe that the Mexican people would allow the Mexican government to settle the NAFTA on the basis of lower standards of environmental regulation. The fallacy of this impression is demonstrated by the grass-roots environmental movement that has arisen in Mexico at various points along the border with the United States.

Bilateral commissions have dealt actively and intensively with the question of the environment. The agreements that have been reached and the legislation that has been shaped to deal with environmental regulation are not perfect, nor will all groups be amenable to them, but their existence points to a very important difference between the question of the environment and the question of labor. In the area of labor issues, the U.S. elections realigned some priorities and options covered under the NAFTA.

One particular new set of options addresses the question of labor migration. The two sides of the border exhibit significant differences in the definition of this question. In the United States, the question of undocumented immigration is defined as a crime-related phenomenon that requires a law enforcement solution. In Mexico, undocumented immigration is considered an economic, labor-related phenomenon. The two governments bypass each other with definitions that are entirely unconnected, leaving little hope for common ground.

LABOR MIGRATION

President Salinas has suggested for the first time in many years that the discussion of immigration with the Clinton administration is a priority for the Mexican government. Immigration negotiations in this case would be subject to a basic disagreement about the definition of the problem, and also over the right figures to be used. Hoping that an agreement can be reached regardless of these fundamental differences, the Mexican government has initiated a strategy in which the first premise is to verify the credibility of data and scientific information about the costs and benefits of immigration. President Salinas and others have made it clear that both sides must agree upon a set of information that will not become a political football between the two countries. They must also agree to use the data in a reasonable way to rationalize the question of immigration.

One project has been counting, observing, and interviewing a systematic random sample of undocumented immigrants as they cross the border between Mexico and the United States. The most intensive crossing point on the 2,000 mile border is Tijuana. The study began in September 1987, and it operates on Friday, Saturday, and Sunday, when the most intensive crossing takes place.

According to this study, 60 percent of the total number of undocumented immigrants have destinations in the state of California. This number varies during the year, with the highest volume in the summer months and the lowest in December. In the summer of 1991, for example, approximately 1.75 million undocumented immigrants crossed from Mexico into the United States. In December, that number declined to approximately 800,000, a difference of almost one-half.

Illegal immigration is difficult to accurately calculate, but studies like this one can generate some estimates about remittances, which are extremely important for the Mexican economy. In 1991, Mexican workers working in the United States remitted approximately $3.5 billion to Mexico. The origin of migrants is highly concentrated (80 percent come from 10 states in central, western, and northern Mexico), so remittances have a significant impact on the local economies of these migrants.

The study estimates that no significant impact will be felt in the phenomenon of undocumented immigration in the first 5 years after the signing of the NAFTA. In 6 to 10 years, the impact will be no more than a 25 percent reduction of the volume observable today. In 11 to 15 years, the study predicts a maximum reduction of 50 percent. This figure will increase exponentially as time goes on.

The NAFTA's impact over the next five years will be minimal because most of the jobs created in Mexico will require a different skill level than that of the average migrant. The psychological impacts of the NAFTA will register first as people hear that jobs are opening. Although they may not benefit directly from these new jobs, they will hear about them and tend to stay in Mexico. The direct economic impact will register when the creation of jobs begins to create additional labor markets in Mexico. These assumptions are based on certain conditions, that is, if nothing else changes from the present situation.

Undocumented immigration and its related conditions are sensitive issues on both sides of the border. In Europe, there is a general misconception about undocumented immigration. Many seem to believe that surreptitious movement across the border is the unilateral desire of Mexican citizens in that region. It is not well known in Europe that the United States was, until recently, the only country in the world where immigration legislation allowed employers to hire foreigners who had entered in violation of immigration laws. This juridical aberration was corrected in 1986 with the passage of the Immigration Reform and Control Act (IRCA). But IRCA has a loophole, one that makes a mockery of sanctions upon employers of illegal aliens. Americans who hire foreigners must prove, with certain documents, that their workers are in the country legally and have the right to be employed. But American employers are not legally obligated to keep copies of these documents—that is the loophole. Thus, questionable situations place the word of the employer against the word of the INS official or anyone challenging the employer's decision. The most important effect of the IRCA has been a mushrooming of the trade in forged immigration documents. At the inception of the IRCA in 1987, the cost of a forged document in San Diego was about $500. Today that price has fallen to around $10.

This unnatural phenomenon was created by the forces that have made undocumented immigration part of a de facto international labor market, one that responds to the interaction of a demand for cheap labor in the United States and a willing supply in Mexico. Mexico and the United States have established no communication regarding the definition of this phenomenon. Obviously, if the United States were to accept the definition of undocumented immigration as a labor-related phenomenon rather than a crime-related phenomenon, the cost of labor would increase. As a result of the asymmetry of power between the two nations, however, the United States does not have to do that.

This asymmetry remains one of the most complicated elements in the aspirations of integration—aspirations that have already been realized at the border, where the free market has operated for many decades. In Tijuana, for instance, consumers already enjoy the options that are expected to result from the NAFTA, if it is signed. Producers at the border have already seen changes take place in the labor force; certain parts of the labor force are already operating under conditions such as total equality and just-in-time production formulas.

The question of labor migration, in the context of negotiation, could thus be more complex and difficult than negotiations of the NAFTA itself. Economics, social inequality, human rights, politics, and a multitude of other sensitive issues are all related to the question of labor migration in the two countries. Unless the parties find a way to utilize the experience of the NAFTA and view this question in a manner that seeks to establish a rational solution, irrational conditions will continue to prevail. At the same time, border relations will continue to demonstrate the extent to which the Mexican people of this region will take advantage of conditions of free trade.

Finally, the Mexican side of the border, contrary to popular assumption, is not the region with the lowest unemployment or the lowest wages in the country. There are some areas in Mexico, a heterogeneous country, where wages and unemployment are both very low, but the notion that every worker in Mexico is waiting for the right moment to jump across the border is entirely false. The relationship between immigration and the NAFTA is far more complex.

PART V
CANADIAN PERSPECTIVES

14. Canada's Interests and the NAFTA

by Ronald Wonnacott

The effects of the NAFTA on Canada's trade relations will continue to be dominated by the consequences of the NAFTA's precursor, the Canada-U.S. Free Trade Agreement (CUSFTA). The problem for Canada is that its growing national debt has left it without an effective fiscal policy, and the program to end inflation initiated several years ago has therefore been left to the monetary authorities. This has meant higher interest rates, which have put pressure on Canadian industry and raised the value of the Canadian dollar by attracting foreign funds. That, in turn, has put further pressure on trade-related industries precisely when they are being asked to make massive adjustments under the CUSFTA.

UNEMPLOYMENT IN CANADA

In reviewing Canada's response since 1990 to a worldwide recession, it is no surprise that the country has had roughly an 11.5 percent unemployment rate in an economy where the usual rate is 7.5 to 8 percent. What is surprising is that, given the adjustments currently taking place, the rate of unemployment has not been higher.

Canada's export performance accounts for this to some extent. In a generally unencouraging economic picture, investment performance has been relatively good while exports (especially to the U.S.) have done very well, with the best explanation being CUSFTA's opening of the U.S. market. Thus, initial indications are that, without CUSFTA, the Canadian recession would have been even worse.

CANADIAN INTERESTS IN THE NAFTA

Now that the free trade agreement includes Mexico, has Canada been able to further its objectives? In some respects it has. In others, its success has been more limited. Let us look briefly at the high points and pitfalls of the new NAFTA for its northernmost partner.

First and foremost, in terms of benefits the Canadian government was successful in achieving its stated goal of gaining access to a rapidly growing Mexican market on terms as favorable as those of the United States. Canada has also seen the end of the Mexican auto decree, licensing arrangements, and Mexican tariffs. With the exception of markets in milk and feathers (where Canada's decision to protect its markets and opt out of liberalizing trade prompted Mexico to respond in kind), Canada has acquired the same favorable terms of entry into Mexico as has the U.S. That is, by participating in the NAFTA, Canada has avoided the discrimination it would have had to face in Mexico in competing with duty-free U.S. goods.

There is another benefit that has not yet been cited by the Canadian government—Canadian tariff-free access to Mexican supplies of inexpensive goods. This is important for consumers as well as industries using these goods as inputs in order to remain competitive in the world market. Japan has its low-wage sources in Asia; Europe has its low-wage sources in the Mediterranean; it is important that North America also have access to a low-wage source.

Of course, the story is quite different for Canadian firms competing with (rather than using) these Mexican goods. The existence of these firms explains why the Canadian government has not mentioned this issue. Instead, the government emphasizes how it has broken down foreign trade barriers while still maintaining some of its own.

Specifically, Canada has managed to open up the Mexican market in red meat and grains while fully retaining its protection for supply management in milk and feathers. Because this is the kind of deal politicians view as a success, the implication is that a country's own politicians are poor agents for pursuing the national interest. In fact, better agents for this purpose may be the very trading partners putting pressure on the country to reform its domestic policies. A good example of this is the United States' recent threat to increase barriers against French wines in reaction to the French (and, more broadly, European) agricultural subsidy program that damages U.S. exports. This U.S. policy is obviously a very high-risk strategy because it could lead to a trade war. On the other hand, if a policy like this is successful, it means the Americans will have forced upon the French a reform that no French politician would have touched, but which is in the interest of both France and the European Community.

In fact, when you look at the situation this way, the NAFTA is superior to treaties like the General Agreement on Tariffs and Trade. While the GATT has allowed developing countries to maintain many of their own barriers to liberalized imports, the NAFTA has effectively told Mexico (and other future participants) that if they intend to participate, they must be prepared to reduce their own trade barriers. This is very much in the interest of these less developed countries, even though it does put temporary pressure on them.

RULES OF ORIGIN

The NAFTA has also assuaged some irritants to trade between the U.S. and Canada. Clarified rules of origin should reduce the risk of conflicts like the "Honda dispute," in which Honda cars produced in Canada were assessed duty when shipped into the United States because they allegedly did not satisfy rules of origin. The NAFTA has attempted to clear up ambiguities in this area by detailing its rules of origin in some 200 pages.

This change in rules of origin has, however, had unfortunate consequences in autos and in textiles and apparel (where the rules have become more stringent). A firm producing clothing must not only use a North American fabric, but use a fabric that is made with North American yarn.

The problem with tougher rules of origin is that they allow the U.S., the NAFTA country with the largest market, to protect itself not only from countries outside NAFTA, but also from its trading partners within. To illustrate, suppose a Japanese transplant firm is considering a location in the U.S., which is by far its largest North American market. On those U.S. sales, the firm is exempt from any origin requirements. If, however, the Japanese firm is considering a Canadian or Mexican location, it will find that to sell in the U.S. market, it must satisfy rules of origin requirements. The stiffer the NAFTA makes those requirements, the less attractive a Canadian or Mexican location becomes. Of course, the American objective in stiffening these rules was to prevent Mexico from becoming a low-wage platform on which nonmember countries could manufacture products and then ship them duty-free into the U.S. The question for Canada is how much it has been sideswiped in this process. (In compensation, Canada has received an increase in its tariff rate quotas for its clothing shipments to the U.S.)

Another Canadian objective was to cement gains won from the FTA between the U.S. and Canada. Unfortunately, there was one Canadian gain from the CUSFTA that disappeared in the NAFTA (as it would have in any free trade agreement between Mexico and the U.S.): Canada lost its preference over Mexico in the U.S. market because Mexico also gets duty-free access. But Canada still retains its preference over other countries.

ADVANTAGES FOR CANADA OF THE NAFTA OVER CUSFTA

For Canada, the NAFTA is an improvement on the CUSFTA in a number of respects. Canada now has an extension of duty drawbacks and greater discipline over standards, which should reduce border conflicts with the U.S. Perhaps best of all, Canada, the U.S., and Mexico have the same low or zero most favored nation (MFN) tariff on computer imports from non-NAFTA countries. This old customs union model has huge advantages because rules of origin are not required for trade in that product within the union. Administering rules of origin has become a nightmare because of the difficulty in determining what percentage of which product comes from where.

Fortunately, two problems that have led many economists to reject customs unions in the past have been avoided in the harmonization of these computer tariffs. The first is that the weaker partners in a union run the risk of damage to their sovereignty if they have to accept external tariff rates imposed by the more powerful partner. In the NAFTA, this problem does not arise because the new harmonized tariff is not set at the U.S. level, but rather at the lowest common denominator of all the members' tariffs. The second problem is that a common external tariff invites a disguised form of protectionism against outsiders. Once again, this problem was avoided because the new tariff has been set so low. Perhaps this progress in the computer industry can be extended to other industries as well.

A final Canadian objective was to ensure that the U.S. does not get a location advantage over Canada. If Canada were not a participant in the NAFTA, it would have faced a hub-and-spoke trading system in which the U.S. would have one bilateral free trade agreement with Canada and another with Mexico and would be the only country to be a participant in both. In other words, only a firm located in the United States would have free access to all three markets. A Mexican or Canadian location would limit the firm to free trade in only two markets.

The hub-and-spoke problem runs far deeper than this. If Canada had not participated in the NAFTA, the U.S. might, by adding more spoke binationals, have been able to carve up the hemisphere in a series of discriminatory bilateral agreements. In such an environment, Canadian industry would have become less and less able to compete with American industry. Canada's incentive to participate in the NAFTA was not so much the advantages of getting in—although these advantages are likely to be substantial—but rather the avoidance of problems associated with staying out.

15. The Development Impact of the NAFTA: A Canadian Perspective

by Ann Weston[1]

I will concentrate my comments in three areas: first, the lessons that may be drawn from the Canadian experience with the Canada-U.S. Free Trade Agreement (CUSFTA); second, the implications for Mexico and other countries in the hemisphere contemplating NAFTA membership; and third, the implications for other developing countries.

CANADIAN EXPERIENCE: A CAUTIONARY TALE?

For many Canadians, evaluation of the NAFTA must be seen through the lens of the Canadian experience under the CUSFTA.

The CUSFTA has not been altogether rosy. Of course the timing was bad, coinciding with macroeconomic problems (overvalued exchange rate, burgeoning government deficit) as well as the global recession, which complicates the analysis.

The CUSFTA was probably oversold. Even the most widely quoted study by the Economic Council (Magun et al., 1988), for example, projected only a 2.5 percent increase in national output after 10 years and a net gain of 251,000 jobs, of which only 19,000 would be in manufacturing. There would be gross job losses of 188,000 and a relatively small share of average annual permanent job losses, most resulting from intra-industry specialization rather than from massive inter-industry restructuring. Net job losses were predicted in 7 industries—including rubber/plastics, leather, textiles, and knitting. However, if forecast productivity gains of 6.1 percent failed to materialize, 17 of the 36 industry groups would face net job losses.

Nonetheless, even the most ardent supporters of the CUSFTA have been taken aback by the rapidity of the restructuring in the Canadian economy. To quote a few statistics:

Unemployment reached 11.6 percent in September 1992 (up from 7.8 percent in 1988), with levels as high as 20 percent in Newfoundland. Even in Ontario it is approaching the national average of 11.3 percent for the first time since 1980. Since 1988, altogether 295,000 jobs have been lost in the economy as a whole, and 400,000 in manufacturing alone. All levels have been affected, but especially blue-collar workers, with more than one in seven unemployed. Bankruptcies in the first six months of 1992—totaling 7,136—almost equaled those recorded for all of 1988.

Competition from U.S. goods and services has increased in several sectors, such as meat/dairy products, clothing, processed foods, furniture and furnishings, and financial services, where there has been liberalization under the CUSFTA.

There has also been an expansion of exports to the U.S., including telecommunications and office equipment, paper, and other crude materials. Even within industries that appear to be downsizing, new niches have been established. One example is a Canadian woolen suit firm, which took advantage of its preferential access over competing European suppliers and made large investments in new technology that significantly expanded its market share.

Nonetheless, there is widespread disenchantment with the experience under the CUSFTA. Besides issues of employment and output, some of this criticism has focused on the failure of the bilateral dispute settlement mechanisms to diminish the incidence of conflicts. Other criticisms have centered on the indirect pressures to harmonize, e.g., the fiscal system and the introduction of the Goods and Sales Tax (GST), labor standards, and intellectual property laws. These are not addressed here for reasons of brevity.

Considerable criticism has been directed at the government's response, notably the failure to introduce complementary policies that might ease the adjustment costs and assist firms and especially workers to take advantage of the new opportunities. There has been a reorientation from passive ("safety net") to more active ("trampoline") policies, following some of the recommendations of the De Grandpré report in 1989 (Advisory Council on Adjustment, 1989). Generally, however, training program availability is well below levels in the European Community, and access to unemployment insurance has been reduced.

Nor has there been an active industrial or technology policy to assist the adjustment of firms. The failure of the CUSFTA to define acceptable subsidies, and thus the continued fear of U.S. trade action, may have chilled government intervention in support of ailing industries (Doern and Tomlin, 1991; Campbell, 1992).

A consensus has begun to emerge about the need for something more. For instance, a C.D. Howe Institute Commentary (Schwanen 1992) concludes that "the painful restructuring that has occurred in certain sectors under the CUSFTA suggests that the issue of adjustment programs should be revisited." There are various views about what form an adjustment program might take, and whether it should be entrenched in law, specifically in the NAFTA.

These demands for adjustment assistance are growing in the face of the NAFTA even though most analyses conclude that it will have a small impact (maybe negative, maybe positive) on the Canadian economy. For example, a report issued by the Department of Finance (1992) estimated that the NAFTA would likely raise GDP in Canada by only 0.03 percent compared to 0.07 percent in the U.S. and 2 percent in Mexico.[2] This small increase in GDP largely reflects the limited economic linkages between Canada and Mexico. The major challenge will be in the U.S. market, where there is already evidence of increasing similarity of Canadian and Mexican markets—in fact, the similarity index of Mexican and Canadian exports to the U.S. more than doubled from 16 percent in 1971 to 34 percent in 1987.

Again it is important to disaggregate the effects of the distribution of costs and benefits of the NAFTA within, as well as between, the three economies. Improved monitoring and evaluation of the impact of the NAFTA seem an essential first step toward better understanding of the adjustment process and appropriate policy responses. Canada has agreed to monitor labor and environmental standards in Mexico, but not domestically. A number of Canadians have called for monitoring of working conditions and of the adequacy of adjustment policies in all three countries (similar to suggestions by Hufbauer and Schott, 1992, for example). Howse (1992) recommends creating permanent national adjustment councils, which would report to a trinational body.

The issue of enforcement of both adjustment measures and labor standards has been raised in Canada. Some favor a social charter, deriving from the EC experience. For example, Howse proposes that a social charter be attached to the NAFTA that would include the right to adjustment assistance for all displaced workers. The assistance would be provided through training subsidies or programs, job search facilities, relocation assistance, income maintenance, and mandatory notice periods for plant closings, though each NAFTA member would have the flexibility to choose its own policy mix.

In this case, the NAFTA would have to exempt any adjustment support from trade remedy action; in some cases, however, it may be difficult to distinguish measures introduced to promote adjustment and those designed to protect an industry. Moreover, the NAFTA should require compliance with these provisions before any safeguards could be introduced. This would remedy the present asymmetry whereby firms (or workers) may seek protectionist redress but not positive adjustment assistance, thus helping to defuse tensions both within and between countries.

Proposals for enforcement of adjustment and labor standards range from the negative (withdrawal of right to protection to withdrawal of preferred market access) to the positive (access to a regional development fund, building on the EC policy of social cohesion funds and regional development assistance). For instance Brown et al. (1992) recommend a 5 percent diminishing fee imposed on all flows of goods, services, and capital, which would generate some $20 billion. Others (e.g., Hufbauer and Schott, 1992; and Howse, 1992) argue that national governments should be primarily responsible for adjustment, though Howse favors the creation of a trinationally financed emergency relief fund, supported by tariff revenues, for use where government policy is lacking.

IMPLICATIONS FOR MEXICO AND OTHER COUNTRIES IN THE HEMISPHERE

The failure of the NAFTA to include specific adjustment-related provisions—at least to date—is probably all the more serious when viewed from the position of Mexico and other prospective NAFTA members.

Much of the literature about trade liberalization in developing countries now endorses the crucial political and economic roles to be played by complementary adjustment policy in addressing rigidities in labor, capital, and technology markets. A World Bank (1988) study of Mexico found that employment was slow to respond to trade liberalization. Training and credit programs may be essential to ensure that the benefits of trade liberalization are quickly realized, especially by smaller and medium-sized firms, which otherwise risk being marginalized (Vega and Castillo, 1991). A study on Mexican agriculture concluded that "there are substantive reasons for concern about the distributional impact of agricultural liberalization in the absence of proper adjustment policies" (Levy and Wijnbergen, 1991, p. 25).

If the NAFTA fails to deal directly with the adjustment issues likely to arise in Mexico, does the agreement provide special rules sensitive to Mexico's different level of development and the greater adjustment entailed in its liberalization? These rules, for instance, might allow the government to continue stipulating that foreign investors transfer technology, or use public procurement to promote development of backward regions, or subsidize agricultural diversification. Second, does the phasing and extent of liberalization in particular sectors allow for asymmetric or relative reciprocity (Salazar and Lizano, 1992)?

Although draft versions of the NAFTA text (e.g., the "Dallas" text leaked in Canada in February 1992) spoke the familiar GATT language of special and differential treatment, this had disappeared by September 1992 when the final legal text was released. Instead, the NAFTA is presented as an agreement between equals—"partners in power" according to Maclean's (December 14, 1992)—with each accepting essentially the same rules and obligations. There are some exceptions, notably the exclusion of parts of the energy sector from Mexico's obligations.

All three countries have grandfathered exceptions to the public procurement provisions, but for Mexico this list appears more extensive. In some cases, Mexico will be granted a slightly longer phase-in period, such as three years for intellectual property rights (though this is less than the five years proposed in the GATT Dunkel text). Mexico may receive technical assistance, e.g., for implementing new notification procedures for public procurement.

In some sectors, Mexico has sought to address its particular sensitivities through a longer phase-in period for meeting the common rules. Often this type of concession has been matched by a more gradual opening of the U.S. or Canadian markets.

Consider the case of agriculture. Mexico paid for its reluctance to expose its corn producers to unlimited competition from U.S. and Canadian supplies within 15 years by waiting an equal period before gaining unfettered access to the U.S. market for fruit and vegetables. Asymmetrical phasing on development grounds might have involved more rapid opening of the U.S. market—thus easing the difficult process of adjustment predicted for Mexico's agricultural sector (Levy and Wijnbergen 1991, for example).

In other areas where Mexico would be most able to expand exports and employment rapidly—such as labor-intensive products like clothing and electronic items—sensitivities in the U.S. and Canada have led to more gradual liberalization. Tariffs on clothing will be removed over 10 years (though quotas will be eliminated immediately—a major advance on the Dunkel text, which envisages a 10-year phase-out for quotas). Further, there will be restrictions on this access in the form of strict rules of origin (discussed further below). In the case of glasses, there is asymmetry in favor of the U.S., which has a 15-year phase-out for its tariff, whereas Mexico has only 10 years.[3]

A compensating feature for Mexico (and of interest to other developing countries) may be the special provisions (Article 1021) for small businesses in all three countries. Joint programs will be established and a trinational committee on small business created to promote procurement opportunities for these businesses through programs such as training. A data base of these businesses will be set up for procurers. Efforts will also be made to identify small businesses interested in trading with similar organizations in other NAFTA countries.

In general, however, Mexico is agreeing to abide by the same rules as Canada and the U.S., severely limiting the government's freedom to intervene in the economy whether in regulating investment or public procurement. These limits likely will be tightened further in consultations over procurement by state and provincial bodies, which the NAFTA proposes holding in two years.

Mexico is already moving away from a strong interventionist style of economic management, but the question remains as to whether these new commitments will constrain its development efforts.[4] Many other countries in the hemisphere are also moving in this direction, but several are considerably less developed than Mexico and may, for example, need to maintain greater latitude to control the flow of remittances. Has Mexico raised the stakes too high for them to be able to join the NAFTA?

IMPLICATIONS FOR OTHER DEVELOPING COUNTRIES

There are three main concerns for other developing countries. First, will the NAFTA be inward looking, resulting in significant trade and investment diversion? Second, will it raise the stakes for them by creating new demands in return for market access to North America? Finally, will it weaken the already fragile multilateral system?

In the CUSFTA, trade and investment diversion for third countries—let alone developing countries—was essentially dismissed in a footnote reference (see Magun et al., 1988). Various actors suggest that it is an issue which should be revisited in the NAFTA.

(1) Preliminary (and still somewhat crude) evidence from 1989-91 Canadian import statistics suggests that there has been diversion from the rest of the world, especially in product categories generally produced by developing countries. For instance, Canadian imports of clothing from the U.S. rose 73.5 percent, compared to 4.9 percent from the rest of the world, while growth for furniture and furnishings was 75.6 percent and 1.5 percent,

TABLE 1

Changes in Canadian Imports, 1989-91

Product	Value (1991, $bn)	% Imported from U.S.	% Change in Imports from U.S.	% Change in Imports from ROW
Products Liberalized Under the CUSFTA				
Meat/dairy products	1.059	60	86.2	1.7
Furniture/furnishings	1.880	64	75.6	1.5
Clothing	3.462	10	73.5	4.9
Processed foods/beverages	3.472	49	50.7	3.2
Other household goods	3.072	40	46.7	16.0
Steel	2.364	60	–28.7	51.2
Total including others	79.769	62	14.0	2.8
Products Not Liberalized Under the CUSFTA				
Total	14.594	–70	–8.2	4.4
Services Liberalized Under the CUSFTA				
Total	7.855	71	–12.5	2.4
Services Not Liberalized Under the CUSFTA				
Total	4.441	71	23.6	6.3

Source: Derived from Daniel Schwanen, "Were the Optimists Wrong on Free Trade? A Canadian Perspective," *Commentary No. 37* (Toronto: C.D. Howe Institute, 1992).

respectively. In the case of services, the picture is somewhat cloudy—imports from the United States outpaced those from the rest of the world even more in categories unaffected by the CUSFTA. More details are given in Table 1.

(2) A recent antidumping case gives further ground for concern about third country exports being "crowded out" of North American markets. The NAFTA provides for the exclusion of imports from a partner from any safeguard action taken under GATT Article XIX, when partners are not in the top five suppliers. This could lead to greater restrictions being imposed on third countries in order to achieve a certain level of protection. It is not clear, however, whether this "crowding-out effect" will be greater than under the CUSFTA when the exclusion of partners depended

on their accounting for less than 5 to 10 percent of imports. In practice, there has been little use of Article XIX in recent years, although there has been greater use of antidumping duties (ADD). While in these cases neither the NAFTA nor the CUSFTA provides grounds for exclusion, the access to special dispute settlement procedures may lead to special treatment.[5]

In a recent case involving waterproof rubber footwear, the Canadian International Trade Tribunal recommended (October 1992) that ADD be extended for another four-year period on imports from Czechoslovakia (accounting for 37 percent of imports), as well as Korea, China, Hong Kong, Malaysia, Taiwan, Yugoslavia, and Poland. As competition from countries hit by ADD has fallen, imports from the U.S. facing no ADD grew to the largest single share at 40 percent of imports, which was a 7 percent increase in domestic market share.[6]

Another reason for attaching more importance to antidumping cases is that the duties they involve are often considerably higher than most favored nation (MFN) or generalized system of preferences (GSP) tariffs. Thus, while tariff preferences may be small, there may be significant trade diversion as a result of antidumping duties.

(3) With greater similarity between developing country exports to the U.S. (or Canada), and Mexican exports than Canadian or U.S. exports, many developing countries are concerned that including Mexico in the NAFTA will further displace third country and developing country imports. For instance, 40 percent of Korean exports to the U.S. fall into the same categories as Mexican exports to the U.S. (Kim and Weston, 1993), and this share is rising with the rapid expansion of the range of Mexican manufactured exports. Second, the preferential margin being granted to Mexico is greater than that granted by the U.S. and Canada to each other. It should be noted that longer phase-in of U.S. and Canadian tariff cuts for Mexico will cushion the trade diversion shock.

(4) Several of the NAFTA provisions are more inward looking than similar provisions in the CUSFTA. This is well-illustrated by the complex and detailed rules of origin—many of them tougher under the NAFTA than under the CUSFTA—designed to limit the extent to which third country suppliers take advantage of the free trade area. In some respects, therefore, they parallel the common external tariff adopted by members of a customs union, but they are much less transparent, and thus harder to evaluate. Also, they tend to affect suppliers of inputs rather than final products, though U.S. concerns about Japanese firms using Mexico as a platform for re-export of essentially Japanese products to the

U.S. were behind the negotiation of stringent minimum value-added requirements. (Likewise, some Canadians had raised questions in the CUSFTA debates about Mexican products getting into Canada via the U.S.)

The value-added minimum ranges from 50 percent to 62.5 percent of costs and, in almost all cases, a change in tariff heading, subheading, or even eight-digit tariff heading is also required. In electronics, for example, the number of items with a cost rule is considerably greater than in the CUSFTA. The rules are also much tougher for clothing, an area in which many developing countries have an interest. In the NAFTA, most products have a "yarn-forward" rule, meaning they must be made from North American cloth made from North American yarn, whereas the CUSFTA merely stipulated the use of North American fabric. For most yarns, a "fibre-forward" rule exists.

In autos, minimum North American content rose by 10 percentage points to 50 percent under the CUSFTA and has been further raised to 62.5 percent for cars, light trucks, and their engines/transmissions, and to 60 percent for other vehicles and their components. This is below the 75 percent sought by some groups, while an additional national content rule (e.g., 50 percent Canadian for goods sold in Canada) was excluded. But the rules will be strictly enforced, ending the earlier acceptance of "roll-up" provisions.

Such stringent rules of origin have two contradictory effects on third countries. On the one hand, by limiting the extent to which Mexico (and Canada) may increase its exports to the U.S., they reduce the diversion of trade for final products from third countries. On the other, they reduce North American use of inputs from third countries, an issue of concern for less developed country suppliers of fabric, auto parts,[7] and color TV tubes.[8]

A third key area for many developing countries will be agriculture. Several producers in South America and the Caribbean will be concerned about Mexico gaining preferential access to the highly protected U.S. sugar market, in addition to the market for fruits and vegetables where it already has a strong locational advantage. However, the 15-year period over which quotas are converted to tariffs and then reduced could provide a longer breathing space than had been expected.

There are several other instances where the NAFTA will increase the discrimination against third countries. For example, the preferential opening of services could lead Mexico to displace other suppliers of professional services in the U.S. market, e.g., nurses from the Caribbean. The rules for investment will both discriminate in favor of North American investors and, together with the tariff provisions, increase their incentive to invest in Mexico rather than in other developing countries.

There may be some offsetting spillover effects for third countries, as import demand within North America rises with incomes and as protectionist pressures drop with restructuring and greater competitiveness. For NAFTA members with high tariffs on inputs, there may be pressure for tariff cuts to bring costs in line with other members. For instance, in the December 1992 mini-budget, the Canadian finance minister announced that MFN tariffs on textiles would be brought in line with those of other industrialized countries. Yet adjustment to intra-regional trade could also lead some sectors to resist further extra-regional liberalization.

An early end to the Uruguay Round would help to reduce possible trade diversion as well as allay fears of inward-looking regionalism. However, significant MFN tariff and nontariff barriers will remain, particularly in products of interest to developing countries. Griffin and Khan (1992) suggest that safeguards are needed to ensure that regional blocs do not become inward looking with strong adverse effects on developing countries. Where regional blocs cannot be open to the rest of the world, they should at least be asked to grant preferences, in the form of exemptions from common external tariffs, to exports from poor countries. For example, Griffin and Kahn suggest an international agreement could be reached under the auspices of the United Nations to permit free entry into all Organization for Economic Cooperation and Development (OECD) markets of those products in which poor, labor abundant economies have a comparative advantage.

The new trade policy review mechanism of the GATT could also play a role. Traditionally, FTAs have been reviewed to ensure that they meet the requirements of GATT Article XXIV, but these are generally considered both too general and generous. The review mechanism could help to ensure that FTAs are open by regularly evaluating their impact on third countries and recommending alternative policies as appropriate. This function will be all the more important as regional agreements proliferate and account for a growing share of world trade.

Notes

1. With thanks to Han Soo Kim.

2. Two conflicting estimates for jobs are Hufbauer and Schott (1992) and Waverman (1991)—with the former predicting net Canadian job losses and

the latter job gains. But both estimates are small and based on rough calculations of changes in trade flows rather than on any sophisticated modeling.

3. In general, it is argued that Mexico has been granted a longer timetable. Only 41 percent of its nonoil imports will be liberalized in year 1, another 18 percent in year 5, 38 percent in year 10, and very sensitive items like maize and beans in year 15. In contrast with the United States, 84 percent of Mexican exports to the U.S. will be free in year 1, 8 percent in year 5, 7 percent in year 10 and very sensitive items like sugar and orange juice in year 15. But many of the items to be freed in year 1 are already duty free—as much as 30 percent of all Mexican exports. So the extent of actual liberalization in year 1 is more similar than the initial figures suggest.

4. The Office of Technology Assessment report on U.S.-Mexico trade (1992) notes that expansion of the Mexican electronics industry will require state-led programs to provide education, but also to attract foreign investment and to encourage them to transfer technology, e.g., through limited forms of managed trade, investment controls, or tax credits (p. 171). Such policies might contravene the NAFTA.

5. This suggestion is quite contentious and involves an area requiring further research—given that several analysts have criticized the failure of the CUSFTA and the NAFTA to provide member countries with exemption from trade remedy action.

6. Because of earlier ADD action dating from 1979 for some countries, there have been no Canadian imports from Poland or Yugoslavia since 1987; Korea's share has fallen from 32 percent to 5 percent during this period; Hong Kong has never supplied more than 1 percent of imports, China never more than 4 percent; and Taiwan's share has fallen to 1 percent. Total Canadian sales have decreased, but the domestic industry's share of sales has risen by 11 percent since 1987 to 69 percent, exports to the United States have risen, and the industry is considered profitable. This leads one to question whether the ADD is necessary at all (Canadian International Trade Tribunal, 1992).

7. As the official NAFTA Manual notes, "the new rules of origin for trade in North America will improve opportunities for Canadian auto parts manufacturers faced with growing pressure from low-cost suppliers in Brazil and South East Asia" (Government of Canada, 1992).

8. Office of Technology Assessment, 1992, p. 170, notes that the origin rules prejudice South East Asian tube producers that previously supplied TV producers in Mexico.

Bibliography

Advisory Council on Adjustment (1989). *Adjusting to Win*. Ministry of Supply and Services, Ottawa.

Brown, G., et al. (1992), "Making Trade Fair." *World Policy Journal*, Spring.

Campbell, B. (1992). *Canada Under Siege. Three Years into the Free Trade Era.* Canadian Centre for Policy Alternatives, Ottawa, January.

Canadian International Trade Tribunal (1992). Review No. RR-92-001, October.

Department of Finance (1992). *The North American Free Trade Agreement: An Economic Assessment from a Canadian Perspective.* Ottawa.

Doern, B. and B. Tomlin (1991). *Faith and Fear. The Free Trade Story.* Stoddart, Toronto.

Government of Canada (1992). *North American Free Trade Agreement. An Overview and Description.* Ministry of Supply and Services, Ottawa. August.

Griffin, K. and A.R. Khan (1992). *Globalization and the Developing World: An Essay on the International Dimensions of Development in the post-Cold War Era.* United Nations Research Institute for Social Development, Geneva.

Howse, R. (1992). "The Case for Entrenching a Right to Adjustment in a NAFTA." Faculty of Law, University of Toronto. Mimeo.

Hufbauer, G. and J. Schott (1992). *North American Free Trade: Issues and Recommendations.* Institute for International Economics, Washington, D.C.

Kim, Han Soo and A. Weston (1993). "A North American Free Trade Agreement and East Asian Developing Countries." *ASEAN Economic Bulletin,* Singapore. Forthcoming.

Levy, S. and S. van Wijnbergen (1991). *Labor Markets, Migration and Welfare: Agriculture in the Mexico-US Free Trade Agreement.* World Bank, Washington, D.C. Mimeo.

Magun, S., et al. (1988). *Open Borders. An Assessment of the Canada-US Free Trade Agreement.* Economic Council of Canada, Ottawa. Discussion Paper No. 344.

Maclean's. Toronto, December 14, 1992.

Office of Technology Assessment (1992). *US-Mexico Trade: Pulling Together or Pulling Apart.* Washington, D.C.

Salazar-Xirinachs, J.M. and E. Lizano (1992). "Free Trade in the Americas: A Latin American Perspective." In S. Saborio, editor, *The Premise and the Promise: Free Trade in the Americas.* Overseas Development Council, Washington, D.C.

Schwanen, D. (1992). "Were the Optimists Wrong on Free Trade? A Canadian Perspective." *Commentary No. 37.* C.D. Howe Institute, Toronto. October.

Vega, G. and G. del Castillo (1991). "Comparative Analysis of Mexican and Canadian Manufacturing Firms' Views on North American Free Trade." IDRC, Ottawa. Mimeo.

Waverman, L. (1991). "A Canadian Vision of North American Economic Integration." In Steven Globerman, editor, *Continental Accord: North American Economic Integration.* The Fraser Institute, Vancouver.

World Bank (1991). *World Bank for Trade Policy Reform.* Washington, D.C.

World Bank (1988). *Mexico: Trade Policy Reform and Economic Adjustment.* Washington, D.C, August. Mimeo.

PART VI

INDUSTRY AND LABOR PERSPECTIVES

16. A Businessman's View of the Hemisphere in the 1990s

by John D. Tessier

I would like to present four important changes taking place in the 1990s and then draw some conclusions from these changes. First, global power dynamics have changed, providing an unprecedented opportunity for new perspectives on hemispheric affairs. Secondly, the Latin American countries have implemented dramatic changes in their political and economic systems. Next, the global marketplace has emerged and is reshaping our institutions. Finally, business organizations are becoming more active in the international marketplace and should become better informed and involved in trade and investment negotiations.

IBM IN LATIN AMERICA

Let me discuss these four concepts using IBM's own operations and experience in Latin America as a reference point. Our first Latin American operation started over 70 years ago, and we are now represented in 17 Spanish speaking countries and Brazil. The Central American countries and the Dominican Republic are managed through our affiliate, General Business Machines. Our Latin American operations are profitable, and at the end of 1992, we employed 10,000 people. This year's revenues are expected to exceed $3 billion. We sell and service virtually the complete range of IBM products through 86 marketing and service locations complemented by more than 400 independent dealers and agents who market products such as IBM personal and mini-computers.

We have plants in Martinez, Argentina; Sumare, Brazil; and Guadalajara, Mexico. These plants have a combined annual output of over $800 million, and a broad range of IBM equipment

Note: This paper discusses my personal opinions, which may not represent those of the IBM Corporation.

is exported primarily to other Latin American countries, but also to North America and the Asia-Pacific region, including Japan. Strategically located education, software development, industry application, and scientific centers support the unique needs of the Latin American environment.

THE CHANGING GLOBAL DYNAMICS

The fall of communism has brought about great change in national priorities and perspectives. Security is no longer the overarching concern, and the bipolar world dominated by the military-industrial complex is being replaced by policies focused on economic and social affairs. The Soviet Union has disintegrated and is consumed with its own internal struggle for survival, while the United States, financially overextended by the arms race, is struggling to remake itself and find a new vision for the future.

Economic competition is replacing the Cold War, and the new battleground is the marketplace. No country holds hegemony, but the formula for managing this new environment still alludes us. The GATT Uruguay Round negotiations do not look promising, nor are the G-7 countries cooperating in harmonizing their macroeconomic monetary or fiscal policies. Further, it is too early to know whether the development of trade blocs will ease or make more difficult international trade and capital movements. However, regional trade and investment treaties such as the EC, EEA, NAFTA, MERCOSUR, Andean Pact, and Group of 3 (or is it 4?), are all examples of how global business affairs are evolving.

With the U.S. in transition and searching for its new role, and Latin America increasingly stable and outward looking, there has never been a better time for a period of renewed and strong cooperation in the hemisphere.

LATIN AMERICAN DEVELOPMENT

Inflation, devaluations, economic mismanagement, and mounting foreign debt have made Latin America a challenging environment. In addition to these challenges, businessmen have had to face economic nationalism practiced by several governments until quite recently. Import substitution policies manifested through the imposition of import licensing, restrictive investment procedures, lack of or inadequate intellectual property rights and protection, performance requirements, high tariffs and taxes, and limited remittance procedures were the usual prescription, thus severely limiting foreign assistance. Approximately 6 million new jobs must be generated every year to provide for Latin America's growing population, but the region has insufficient domestic capital formation to generate the needed jobs.

Over the past few years, however, freely elected and democratic Latin American governments have recognized the ineffectiveness of these policies. We have seen the initial efforts to privatize state-owned businesses, deregulate bureaucratic procedures, lower business and dividend taxes, and remove many nontariff barriers, and we have had to recognize that intellectual property protection and enforcement is the price that must be paid for technology transfer and investment.

This trend is a positive one, and we expect it to continue, partly because of the lack of a creditable alternative. Bolivia, Chile, Costa Rica, Mexico, and now Argentina have already progressed quite far along this path. With these countries leading the way and Brazil, Colombia, and Venezuela following, we are witnessing the return to positive economic growth and a more affluent period for Latin America.

Brazil has been struggling with a series of interrelated problems. This Latin American giant holds much promise, but it is still searching for its own unique formula for success. With the continuing shuffling of its economic team, imminent referendum on governance, review of the 1988 constitution, presidential elections in 1994, and an irascible president now in power, it is doubtful that much real progress will be made until a new and hopefully vital president is elected in 1995.

Although 1993 looks to be a year of modest economic growth, because Brazil is struggling out of a three-year long recession, IBM forecasts a 3-3.5 percent aggregate economic growth rate for Latin America, and maybe over 4 percent growth from 1994 to 1996—still well below the Asian newly industrializing countries (NICs). Population growth is expected to continue to moderate around an annual rate ranging from 2 percent to 2.2 percent in the 1990s. If both these estimates are achieved, sustained real economic growth per capita will result and provide an improved standard of living for Latin America's people.

Although Chile took the lead in opening its economy, and made excellent progress during the 1980s, Mexico provides the best example of what is happening in the region. The economic policy transformation under way in Mexico represents broad business opportunities. For example, vast improvements need to be made in the infrastructure, including the education system, the construction of highways, railroads, sea- and airports, and the communications network. Many of these changes will be accelerated by privatization. Each of these areas provides significant opportunities for U.S. and Canadian vendors.

President Salinas' request in September 1991, to negotiate a free trade agreement is another example of changing attitudes. Pragmatism has a strange way of cutting through traditional thinking, and the idea of joining these three economies, together, makes a great deal of sense. The U.S., Canadian, and Mexican economies are quite complementary and should prove to be an excellent fit. Mexico has great natural wealth and a large, hardworking labor force, eager to develop its skills. Mexico's population will approach 100 million by the end of the century and will prove to be voracious consumers, if per capita income picks up in the years ahead as forecasted.

The trend toward democracy and economic liberalization in Mexico, and other Latin American countries, is good news for U.S. and Canadian business as well as for Latin America. It will translate into more jobs, economic and political stability, and a better standard of living for all, as well as increased trade and additional investment opportunities for all alert businessmen.

Canada, with over 25 million people, is the United States' leading trading partner. Latin America, with more than 450 million people, surely offers dramatic possibilities of its own for greatly expanded investment opportunities and trade for both countries.

Perhaps this thought was shared by U.S. government planners when they developed the concept in June 1990 known as the Enterprise for the Americas Initiative, resting on three pillars—debt, investment, and trade. Although it is early in President Clinton's term, initial indications are mixed. He has stated that he favors closer ties with Mexico and all the Latin American countries, and his interpretation of the vision adds a fourth pillar—a social framework. But with pressures on the national budget, it appears the concessionary debt feature has suffered from budget cuts, so we do not really know what lies ahead. My prescription would be that the fourth leg of this accord should be security—but in the widest context—including drug management, human rights, strategic resources, and defense.

The most exciting element of the plan is the U.S. proposal to form a free trade zone throughout the hemisphere. If such a plan is implemented, and there are many thoughtful commentators who believe it is possible, the Western Hemisphere, with 30 percent of the world's land mass and known natural resources, over 25 percent of its gross national product, but only 15 percent of its population, would constitute the largest integrated market in the world. The potential for expansion would be great as the

Latin American countries accelerate economic growth and their economies reap the benefit of regional industrial integration.

THE GLOBAL MARKETPLACE

A more open political environment, seven successful GATT Rounds, the emergence of a worldwide capital market, real-time, satellite supported communications systems, and efficient intercontinental distribution systems have made the global marketplace a reality. Capital, goods, and for the most part businessmen and professionals can operate efficiently and effectively across national borders with fewer restrictions than even three years ago.

The hierarchical organizational approach that developed in the early days of mass production, inherited from the military management system, cannot support the responsiveness demanded by this new, highly competitive environment. Companies in industry after industry have had to focus on areas of core competency, streamline staff levels by cutting out layers of management, out-source some requirements, and restructure their business, delegating management to emancipated, entrepreneurial executives.

Although 18 million new jobs were created during the 1980s, employment growth has been in the small and medium-sized firms. The Fortune "500" suffered net losses in staff as the constituent companies hastily reorganized to increase competitiveness.

Restructuring operations abound as industries have "downsized" and reorganized. Airlines, air-frame, and automobile manufacturing, financial services, steel and our own industry are just a few examples of this worldwide phenomenon.

With markets opening and the internationalization of the Latin American economies, the reorganization of domestic companies, heretofore so massively protected, can only be a matter of time if these organizations are to prosper in the 1990s and provide the productivities and efficiencies these economies need so desperately to survive.

The private sector is not alone. The demand for more adequate social services and other infrastructure, the need to service high national external and internal debt levels, and the importance of balancing national budgets all demand the redirection of spending and more efficient management of public resources on a worldwide basis.

These factors provide strong incentives to redirect and reduce bloated government bureaucracies. More efficient tax collection procedures and privatization all support public cash flows, but public sector overemployment must be addressed. Government must cease to be the employer of last resort. This will place even more pressure on all our governments to spur economic growth, improve the education system, and introduce better retraining systems.

THE PRIVATE SECTOR'S RESPONSIBILITY IN THIS NEW ENVIRONMENT

As we move forward into the 1990s, our leaders will need to rationalize the relationship between the public and private sectors. Especially under a corporate system, business tends to be an extension of government and subject to its wishes and whims.

In an open economic system, the private and public sector roles must be separated, as should labor and investors, each representing their different perspectives, needs, and potential contributions.

Bilateral and multilateral trade and investment relationships require internal dialogue to be expanded to accommodate the interests of all parties in all the effected markets. Governments have the responsibility for negotiating the formal treaties, and understanding the need of their own private sector, by having dialogue with industry associations and geographic chambers. However, there also need to be bi- and multilateral discussions between the business leaders of each affected market, who better understand the complex nature of international business and financial transactions. Public policy can be a very blunt instrument, and potential sanctions arising from a lack of proper understanding should be avoided wherever possible.

Trade associations tend to be adversarial because the members are also competitors. Another successful vehicle for providing input is the binational business council, which brings together cross-industry entrepreneurs from two or more trading nations to discuss common, broad issues, reach a consensus, and then take mutually agreed positions to their respective government officials. In the process, trust and understanding are built, issues and positions are clarified, and overall bilateral relations improved.

IBM Latin America strongly supports such initiatives and considers the Mexico-U.S. Business Committee an ideal model for understanding and resolving issues through business-to-business negotiations.

Of course, there are many other institutions providing forums for debate and discussion on public policy, and the Americas Society, Council of the Americas, and the Center for Strategic and International Studies are especially active and articulate examples.

CONCLUSIONS AND ISSUES

We are encouraged by the progress made so far in the Latin American business environment, for both business in general, and the information processing industry. We believe the region will grow rapidly as a market for exports, capital, and technology, particularly for U.S. and Canadian firms.

Latin America is extremely wealthy in terms of natural resources, but has yet to develop its very large potential. Its average annual per capita income is just over $2,000 versus $20,000 for the U.S. and Canada. We have a great sleeping giant to our south, and one we should build closer relations with during the 1990s.

However, we must be realistic. Our neighbors have been very courageous and made some tough decisions to reach their present level of progress. There are twists and turns ahead and many difficulties to be negotiated, so progress will be uneven and disappointments are bound to be encountered. We must keep the vision clearly before us and set achievable goals to support it.

We must all work hard to rescue GATT. This Round is immensely ambitious but also extremely important. It may also be the last. The membership now exceeds 100 and is still growing, and each member has its own agenda. The issues are becoming more complex and highly contentious. For example, trade-related issues such as environment, human and labor rights, and government subsides are being drawn into the negotiations. Until the global community is ready to harmonize public policies, it will be almost impossible to reach agreements.

On the other hand, regional free trade zones are here to stay, and we must ensure they are GATT consistent and not trade fortresses. I believe, following the eventual ratification of the NAFTA, Chile will accede, and then the Central American countries, the Caribbean Islands, Colombia, and Venezuela will join to form a North American/Caribbean Basin free trade zone before the end of the decade. The Southern Cone countries' inclusion will be dependent on what progress Brazil can make over the next three to four years.

On the other hand, the European Community is likely to evolve into an inner group of countries based on monetary and eventual political union, while an outer group of more loosely related countries, including the European Free Trade Association

(EFTA) and the eastern European countries, will be content to form a single trading unit, the EEA.

The global marketplace is sophisticated, and business transactions are more and more complex. Parts and components can cross borders several times before reaching a distant end-user as a finished product. Some services can move across borders embodied in a common laborer or skilled professional, while others are delivered by value-added international telecommunications networks.

Therefore, U.S. and Canadian businessmen must be willing to take the initiative and work together with their Latin American counterparts, get to know them, their business environment, find where agreements and impediments to trade and investment occur, and then consult with their respective governments to facilitate trade and capital flows and technology transfer. Failure to accomplish these objectives results in poor understanding and unfair and faulty treaties.

I hope the picture I have drawn for you leads you to agree the hemisphere will be going through incredible changes, but holds great opportunity for the balance of the decade. Its public and private institutions will bear little resemblance, both in composition and strategies, to those of the 1980s.

We should recognize the changes taking place in our own countries and in the balance of the hemisphere and take pride in the part we have played in helping our neighbors thus far. The U.S. and Canada should remain patient, but focused, friends, formulating policies and actions to complement and support Latin America's movement toward market-oriented economies.

A hemisphere characterized by democratically elected governments pursuing market-oriented economic policies is, in the end, the surest—and least costly—guarantee of peace and security.

17. A Labor Perspective on the NAFTA

by William C. Doherty

The AFL-CIO would like to rename the North American Free Trade Agreement. We think it should be called the North American Fair Trade Agreement, but as it stands now, it is neither free nor fair.

The American labor community feels very deeply about the negative effects of the NAFTA on the American workforce and the American middle class. The AFL-CIO is pleased with the Clinton administrations's economic philosophy, a sentiment apparently shared by a majority of Americans. Some surveys show that as many as two-thirds of the public have registered a rejection of neoliberalism, trickle down economics, and supply-side economics. The NAFTA represents the worst of all three concepts because it does not consider the needs of the American, Mexican, or Canadian workers. Previous administrations turned a deaf ear to the opinions of labor organizations concerning the NAFTA. The Reagan-Bush administration simply refused to follow U.S. law, which required consultation with the American labor movement in the negotiation of trade agreements, to the same extent that it required consultation with American business, academic, and political communities. The American labor movement objected to the NAFTA vigorously during negotiations, and now we hope that corrective measures are taken to make the social aspects of the agreement more palatable.

The labor movement's primary concern is loss of jobs. Previously, the Canadian-U.S. Free Trade Agreement has generated some conflict between the U.S. and Canada over this issue. The Canadian labor movement claims to have lost about 150,000 jobs to locations across the border with the United States. Firms in Canada pay higher taxes for better medical insurance; an expense they can avoid by relocating to the United States under the free trade agreement.

A greater "job" conflict has been generated, however, between American and Mexican labor interests. At this point, we estimate that between 400,000 and 500,000 jobs from 1,700 U.S. multinational corporations have been lost to workers in Mexico, like those in the Maquiladoras. Corporations have exported these jobs for one economic advantage—low wages. The wage differential between the U.S. and Mexico approaches 8 or 10 to 1. Most recently, Smith-Corona of New York has decided to move its manufacturing operation to Mexico. When that happens, no typewriters or word processors will be produced in the United States. Smith-Corona expects to recoup the $15 million cost of transfer in one year as a result of wage savings. The company's wages will go from $15 or $18 an hour, including benefits, to $2 an hour across the border.

Millions of Mexican workers are being attracted to the border, but only a fraction of them are finding employment. Illegal immigration into the United States has increased under the Maquiladora program because most of the Maquila directors hire women, making it difficult for men, particularly older ones, to find jobs. With few opportunities available in the Maquiladoras, they enter the United States illegally.

Working conditions near the border are disgraceful. We suspect that some of the Maquila directors hire underage workers, especially women, in violation of International Labor Organization standards. They allegedly do not pay Mexican minimum wages and do not follow Mexican or American environmental regulations. For example, some furniture stripping companies from California have moved to Tijuana so that they can use an acid that is illegal in this country. Green Giant produces some food in Mexico because it can still use elements of DDT, an illegal substance in the United States. Multinational corporations seeking to escape the scrutiny of American environmental and labor standards exhibit total disregard for the dignity of the Mexican people.

It may be presumptuous to speak for the Mexican people, but eventually they will begin speaking for themselves. The American labor movement is conducting a series of meetings with the Mexican labor movement because both sides are quite unhappy with the NAFTA as it stands. Mexican labor officials claim that negotiations were conducted in secrecy, while American labor officials did not see the agreement until August 1992.

After serious deliberation by our committees, the AFL-CIO has rendered its judgment. A trade agreement with Mexico is not inherently bad. But our relationship with Mexico ought to have the same degree of dignity as that of the European Community's (EC) relationship with the poorer nations of that continent—Greece, Portugal, Spain, and Ireland. The EC is supporting a substantial development plan to raise the economic status of those countries, rather than simply exploiting them for economic gain.

The development fund that is part of the structure of the European agreement is intended to lend money from the wealthier nations of the Community to the four less developed nations for the purpose of improving their infrastructure. Infrastructure, in this case, is an umbrella term that includes projects such as highways, communications systems, and public plant and equipment. Evidently, the European social fund is already generating benefits for the nations it encompasses. Social Security benefits have been standardized for European workers. Workplace regulations, like child labor laws, antidiscrimination policies, and collective bargaining rights, have all been negotiated.

We would like to see this type of progress in U.S.-Canadian-Mexican economic relations. Perhaps the NAFTA can institute a government financial aid plan allowing Mexico to obtain long-term, low-cost credits to improve its infrastructure. Equalization can occur—Mexican workers can have good jobs and a higher standard of living without taking jobs away from American workers who deserve the same things.

Congress has yet to approve the NAFTA. Officials in the Clinton administration, especially Secretary of Commerce Ron Brown and Secretary of Labor Robert Reich, share the American labor movement's commitment to job creation. America must reindustrialize and seek a return to the days of labor-management-government cooperation. These groups have not always been at loggerheads.

Labor must negotiate with management. National economic development plans aside, we must combine our efforts to decide what is good for business and the American workers and how to implement a recovery. Because if business fails, workers lose jobs, and that benefits no one.

There is no such thing as free trade. The NAFTA itself contains some provisions designed to protect American multinationals. Remission of profit, property rights, and intellectual rights are all guaranteed in the NAFTA. The American labor movement would like any trade agreement to include some provisions designed to protect the workers of all three nations—decent Social Security benefits, strict enforcement of labor laws, and rights to freedom of association and collective bargaining.

Labor would like to see trade managed to the benefit of the United States and the other parties to the agreement. On the other hand, we are skeptical of the benefits of dividing the globe into regional trading blocs. Trilateralizing a formerly bipolar world, in our opinion, defeats the purpose of the General Agreement on Tariffs and Trade (GATT). GATT should work to decentralize economic power—to unify the world with a global economy and to increase the standard of living of the citizens of this earth.

The present agreement espouses a terribly unjust and unbalanced approach toward improving our relationship with Mexico. President Salinas has reversed a tradition that was based on creating a fear of Mexico's ugly neighbor to the north. He is moving away from the old monolithic, one-party system of government and holding multiparty elections. Mexico is progressing at a great rate, and the United States should encourage that. The American labor movement does want trade with Mexico, but it must be fair trade. We encourage the development of fair and equitable economic development throughout the Americas. We look forward to the improvement of regional trade if it is to the mutual advantage of all of the nations in the region and if it does not undercut the GATT.

The NAFTA holds more at stake than the profits of multinational corporations. If the name of the game is money, the bottom line can improve without risking social stability, social justice, and true democracy. The Soviet Union failed because the command economy benefitted a few in the top tier and did nothing to encourage popular participation. We do not want to see this happen with trade relations in this hemisphere.

18. The Sector Advisory Process and the NAFTA

by Eugene W. Zeltmann

As Chairman of an Industry Sector Advisory Committee for Capital Goods (ISAC-2), I want to highlight the role of the sector advisory process in the NAFTA negotiations. There are 17 advisory committees representing diverse interests such as telecommunications, agriculture, energy, and textiles. Each of these ISACs, as the committees are called, originated from the 1974 Trade Act that directed government agencies to solicit advice from various sectors of the U.S. business community in the establishment of trade procedures.

The ISAC for capital goods has about 23 members representing concerns such as construction equipment, machine tools, energy-related items, and electrical products. The Committee represents both large and small companies competitive in domestic and international markets. Some of the members, in fact, have had experience in penetrating closed markets and know first-hand the frustration of exclusion and the elation of access.

THE WORK OF ISAC

As a member of ISAC-2, my work is dedicated to removing barriers to the free conduct of trade in capital goods, including the area of heavy electrical equipment. The issue of the NAFTA first arose while ISAC-2 was working on the Uruguay Round of the General Agreement on Tariffs and Trade (GATT); when the government procurement code talks began in earnest, our interest was peaked.

One of the tasks we were asked to undertake was a comprehensive evaluation of the several thousand-page free trade agreement. The Committee then made a presentation to Congress regarding the NAFTA's pluses and minuses. When assessing areas outside our expertise, such as textiles and agriculture, we necessarily deferred to experts in those fields. In the area of capital goods, however, ISAC-2 made several strong suggestions.

ISAC AND THE NAFTA

First of all, we wanted to make it extremely clear that we were loyal proponents of free and open trade. We told Congress that we abhorred trade barriers and believed that the NAFTA would go a long way in eradicating many of these. The removal of trade barriers, we said, "unshackles the creative energies of the people of the three North American signatories."

Government Procurement and Tariffs

During the deliberations, ISAC members addressed two serious concerns: government procurement and tariffs. The issue of government procurement resulted in some fascinating negotiations. As of 1994, the proposed NAFTA will open up bidding on 50 percent of all purchases of Commission Federal des Electricidad (CFE) and Pemex (Mexico's national oil company) annual procurements. That number increases to 55 percent in 1995, 60 percent in 1997, 65 percent in 1999, and 100 percent open bidding in the year 2003. This was a major accomplishment that resulted from tough negotiations. It represents, in our view, a major step toward lowering barriers to free trade.

The other major concern addressed by ISAC members was that of tariffs. Negotiations resulted in a lot of give and take. For example, U.S. tariffs on steam turbines shipped to the United States from Canada or Mexico will fall from 7.5 percent to zero percent on January 1, 1994. Mexican tariffs on imports will decrease from 20 percent to zero percent in five annual stages beginning January 1, 1994. Specifically in regard to combustion turbines, the Mexican and U.S. tariffs of 10 percent and 5 percent respectively will drop to zero percent as of January 1, 1994.

It was these kinds of results that encouraged our ISAC to throw its support behind the NAFTA as we did. We told Congress that although we were disappointed that only a few U.S. capital goods were placed under the NAFTA's A and B categories for quick tariff reduction, the Committee fully supported the agreement. We recognized, of course, that capital goods would eventually receive duty-free treatment.

Environment and Labor Issues

Two other interesting and initially unexpected concerns that arose during our negotiations addressed the NAFTA's impact on the environment and on labor. After further negotiation and study, we decided that after all was said and done, the NAFTA's impact on U.S. employment would be positive. However, for those workers who would lose jobs and be unable to find employment with their current skills, we recommended that assistance and job training in other fields be supplied. To accomplish this, we supported the Bush administration's proposed comprehensive federal program for worker adjustment. This program should contribute $10 billion over a five-year period for worker retraining. It is our conviction that although the NAFTA's benefits will certainly outweigh its drawbacks, those people who are adversely affected must not be forgotten.

I was recently asked why I thought the NAFTA would be good for the power-generation business. The person posing the question was clearly convinced that the NAFTA would result in a net loss of American jobs to Mexico. I responded that in a high-technology business such as power generation, lowered trade barriers will substantially increase opportunities for businesses on both sides of the border. We estimate, for example, that between 1992 and 2001, Mexico will be placing orders for 18,000 megawatts of electric power generation. Some of this will be supplied by large steam turbines, some by combined cycles, and some by simple-cycle gas turbines. My estimated order potential for these 10 years is $2.8 billion. That translates, by our calculations, to approximately 11,000 man-years of work.

These are exactly the high-technology, high-paying jobs that politicians were talking about during the Fall 1992 election campaign in the United States. Because these jobs can potentially benefit U.S. turbine workers in a very substantial fashion, turning our backs on such opportunities made little sense to us.

The environmental issue also drew our attention. It was our view that the NAFTA is indeed a "green agreement" resulting in substantial environmental improvement when implemented. This is obviously the subject of heated debate, but we believe that power-generation provides a good example to support this assertion. Significant improvements in environmental performance can be obtained using today's combined-cycle power-generation plants that utilize natural gas for the production of electricity. These units operate at 55 percent efficiency, perhaps doubling the efficiency levels of existing equipment in many areas. From an environmental viewpoint, the NAFTA helps by greatly reducing chemical emissions: sulphur dioxide emissions are reduced to virtually zero; carbon monoxide to less than 10 parts per million; and oxides of nitrogen to less than 10 parts per million. These numbers are far superior to the emission levels of existing plants.

Our committee recognizes, of course, that the subjects of environment and labor are highly contentious. We, however, are glad that these issues are now being discussed and feel that the NAFTA deals with them in a very appropriate fashion.

Finally, I want to mention the advisory process itself. The fact that it works is evidenced by the increasing number of advisory groups participating in trade talks like the NAFTA or the Uruguay Round. Mexican advisors were particularly active during the NAFTA negotiations and were instrumental in bringing initial negotiations to a close. In contrast, one of the reasons the GATT Uruguay Round negotiations stalled two years ago was because the European business community had no appropriate vehicle through which it could convey its views to the EC negotiators.

With all of this in mind, the first months of the Clinton administration will be a critical time. Many issues will transcend the partisan transfer of power with little or no trouble. However, I am not certain that the NAFTA will be one of these easy issues. Thus, it is imperative that those endorsing the agreement work to ensure that it does not fall by the wayside. Acute political insights and strategies will be required to ensure success.

19. Trade Liberalization and Mexico

by Juan de Nigris

I would like to make three comments about the Mexican workforce and private sector perspectives on free trade. First, I will address the economic and social changes that are taking place in Mexico. Second, I will discuss the NAFTA in the context of these economic and social changes. Finally, I will highlight VITRO's strategy and its experiences with the trade liberalization process.

To begin, I must point out that the socioeconomic changes occurring in Mexico today are not just another result of the country's general economic policy. These changes are taking place rapidly and are having an increasingly profound effect on the Mexican experience.

MEXICO, THE NAFTA, AND THE GATT

A good subject to start this discussion is the General Agreement on Tariffs and Trade (GATT). The liberalization of the Mexican economy began with its entrance into the GATT in 1986. Joining the GATT shifted the impetus for economic growth away from public and toward private investment. It has demanded very difficult fiscal reforms and a sharp reduction in the government's foreign and domestic debt. As a result of its membership in the GATT, Mexico has pursued a powerful privatization process in conjunction with a liberalization process in foreign investment, deregulation, and intellectual property. To top it off, Mexico also has multiple free trade agreements.

The most important of these agreements is, of course, the NAFTA. But Mexico has also signed a free trade agreement with Chile and is in the process of signing others with Central America, Colombia, Venezuela, and the Group of Six. In addition to these agreements, Mexico is pursuing very important social programs of educational reform and community development. However, these developments will not be discussed in detail. I do want to emphasize that NAFTA is only one part of Mexico's economic and social strategy. This last point must be stressed—the NAFTA is about economic growth, but social reform as well.

ECONOMIC GROWTH IN MEXICO

The public deficit is one measure of the degree to which the Mexican economy is changing. This deficit has been reduced from

17 percent to 1.5 percent of GDP in only six years. Although the exchange rate may be slightly overvalued, Mexico has sufficient foreign exchange reserves to comfortably maintain the rate at its current level for some time.

Another measure of change is the rate of inflation. The stabilization program has resulted in a drop in inflation from 180 percent to 16 percent—a remarkable achievement in Latin America. That figure dropped from three digits to barely two and is expected to drop by another 1 percent by next year.

These changes have accompanied Mexico's moderate and stable growth. Currently, the Mexican economy is more dynamic than that of both the United States and Canada.

All of these factors signal renewed confidence. In turn, this confidence invites a decrease in real interest rates and a sizable increase in capital inflows. That means greater exchange rate stability and enhanced benefits for investment in the Mexican economy.

However, it is critical that observers outside Mexico understand the extent of the changes that Mexicans have lived with for the past six years. It has not been an easy task. Those who wanted the Mexican model to transform itself from an interventionist to a market-oriented model in six years have witnessed very good results in a very short period of time. Unfortunately, after making such drastic adjustments and reaping successful results, critics still remind us that we have left several items off the agenda or have failed to perform certain programs—a sure sign that they do not understand what is going on in Mexico. Those who want Mexicans to make more sacrifices or pursue a more rapid transition do not understand Mexican realities.

What we must realize is that not all of Mexico's problems can be solved through the NAFTA. I want to reiterate that while the NAFTA is an important piece of Mexico's economic strategy, it is still only one piece. Attempting to use the NAFTA as a cure-all will only endanger the good results already achieved. Before the NAFTA negotiations began, many people thought the agreement was worthless. But now that the first round of negotiations has ended, everyone wants to put further demands on the NAFTA.

Consider the North American market. It has approximately the same population as the European Community. Also, North American GNP and per capita income are quite close to those of the EC. However, the Mexican GNP is just 4 percent of the U.S. GNP. It is difficult to believe that with this small percentage, Americans perceive that Mexico will damage the U.S. economy, much less determine U.S. macroeconomic policies.

MEASURING THE NAFTA'S BENEFITS

What potential benefits may be created by the NAFTA? There are six negotiating groups participating in the NAFTA: those dealing with market access, trade rules, services, investment, intellectual property, and dispute settlement.

Whether or not the NAFTA successfully addresses these issues, the agreement is not by itself a result of "good" or "bad" negotiating. Rather, it is simply a set of clear rules that define behavior in the regional economy. The NAFTA's results will depend more on the behavior of the region's social actors than the rules. The rules themselves are important because they may inspire confidence for investors in the Mexican, Canadian, and American economies. But the agreement does not assure countries of receiving all of the potential benefits of the NAFTA; we must work very hard to obtain them. For example, the tariff rate in the U.S. will drop, but that does not mean a company will have the capabilities to enter the U.S. market. Regardless of the tariff diminution, standards will have to be met in marketing, retailing, and other areas in order for the change to be effective.

What about country-specific benefits derived from the NAFTA? The dynamism of the Mexican economy combined with its very high propensity to import U.S. goods can greatly benefit the United States. Of each dollar Mexico imports, 75 cents comes from the United States. Of each additional dollar of income generated in Mexico, 15 cents is spent on imports from the United States. These American imports into Mexico will also include critical capital and high-tech goods.

With respect to market access opportunities in Mexico, we have a resource complementarily that is not necessarily labor intensive. We can and do export some high-tech products originating from domestic industry rather than foreign multinationals. In Mexico we have particular opportunities in the automobile, agriculture, and textile sectors.

I have one question regarding trade rules: Can Mexican imports really hurt U.S. industry? Mexican imports to the U.S. represent 2 percent of total U.S. consumption. Yet some U.S. industries are telling us we are not only hurting them, but endangering their very existence. In fact, I believe that the United States will benefit greatly from the Mexican market for U.S. service exports in financial services, transportation, telecommunication, engineering, and other professional services.

In Mexico, one benefit of the NAFTA is that we expect to reduce the protectionist use of safeguards and countervailing and antidumping cases against us. Although we are not sure if we will be able to eliminate these problems, at least we will have more instruments available to avoid them.

In investment, Mexico has a great opportunity to increase the number of joint ventures between Mexicans and foreigners and to promote investment not only from the U.S. and Canada but from nationals in Mexico and investors in the Pacific and Europe.

In the intellectual property sector, the U.S. will benefit greatly. Among other areas, Mexico will want assistance in the pharmaceutical, television, record, and movie industries.

The sixth area of negotiation is dispute settlement. The important question here is whether or not Mexican industry has the financial resources to cover investigation costs. Even though we have the right to dispute settlement, the prohibitive costs of investigation have acted as a sort of tariff for small firms in Mexico. The NAFTA should reduce costs in this area, as well as in the other five already mentioned.

THE EXPERIENCE OF VITRO GLASS

A discussion about the NAFTA can, in my opinion, benefit from the inclusion of a particular company's experience. I work for VITRO, one of the world's top three corporations in the glass-container industry. VITRO is currently the second largest private corporation in Mexico with annual sales in the neighborhood of $3 billion. It employs 45,000 people, 8,000 of whom are in the United States. Glass container production is, in fact, only one segment of VITRO's massive production. It also makes plastic containers, luggage, flat glass for the construction and auto industries, crystal kitchenware and tableware, fiberglass, chemical products, and some capital goods. However, VITRO's main business is by far the manufacturing of flat glass containers, representing 60 percent of total sales.

VITRO is an international company with 53 percent of consolidated sales outside Mexico. Close to 50 percent of our assets are located outside Mexican borders, and we have production facilities in the United States and Central America. Last year, the company's exports from Mexico amounted to more than $350 million.

Over the years, VITRO has created a number of joint ventures with international companies. In 1964, 55 years after its 1909 establishment, VITRO first entered into a joint venture with Comegua, a Guatemalan production facility. One year later, VITRO initiated a joint venture with England's Pilkington, a float-glass production facility. In 1969, VITRO signed a technical assistance agreement with Owens-Illinois, and later entered into a joint venture with its glass container division. In 1976, VITRO was first listed on the Mexican Stock Exchange. 1980 saw VITRO and Ford Motor Company begin a joint venture in the production of windshields to be exported to the United States. In 1986, VITRO began producing luggage for Samsonite Corporation and in 1987, it began making household appliances for Whirlpool. 1989 marked VITRO's acquisition of Anchor Glass. In 1991, WTI and VITRO entered into a joint venture for glassware wholesale with production facilities in the U.S. and the Pacific. In the same year, VITRO was listed on the New York Stock Exchange.

VITRO's glassware division in particular has continued to arrange strategic alliances in order to globalize its operation. In 1992, a division of VITRO entered into a joint venture with Corning's glassware division.

At the same that VITRO has expanded, it has developed numerous social programs for its workers. Among other benefits, VITRO provides education, training, health care, immigration facilities, housing, and food for its employees.

VITRO's experience serves as proof that Mexico has been fighting to achieve and maintain international competitiveness and economic efficiency for a long time. In the process, VITRO has not forgotten its social responsibility. Economic realities show that we can improve our development prospects by ourselves. Mexico has proved it is much more than just an export platform or a big Maquiladora. VITRO is just one company in Mexico; there are many more which have followed the same developmental path. They are all ready to continue with their processes of modernization.

From this perspective, VITRO and other Mexican companies aren't simply reacting to the NAFTA. The 1989 acquisition of Anchor Glass, for example, occurred well before the NAFTA. Mexican companies are reacting to global realities as much as regional ones. We know we have gotten a late start to economic reform and we have been working quickly to take advantage of economic opportunities which began rising well before the NAFTA. We know if we had begun this process in 1970 when the East Asian NICs began, we would be in a very different position now.

I do not want to imply that VITRO is the model of success. Rather, I want to show that Mexicans are indeed trying to reap the benefits of the NAFTA, while continuing to look toward the long run. The NAFTA is more than just a symbol of presidential election politics. Its consequences have been felt beyond the U.S. elections, and will certainly continue to affect us beyond the next

Mexican elections. However, if the realities of the situation are not well understood, the consequences of the NAFTA may be negative for all three "beneficiaries."

PART VII

REGIONAL TRADING BLOCS, SOCIAL POLICIES, AND CROSS-BORDER CONSTITUENCIES

20. Can the EC Social Charter Be a Model for the NAFTA?

by Reiner Hoffmann

If the NAFTA wants to do more than provide a framework for unbounded liberalism that disregards the basic social rights of the working population, it is essential that the social dimension of the American single market be firmly embedded in the provisions of the NAFTA treaty.

Can Europe's experience with social charters be of use to the NAFTA? According to the Bush administration, one of the main reasons for concluding the NAFTA was to ensure that the North American region could continue to compete with the European market. This argument resembles those once put forward by European governments. Their aim was to overcome the problem of so-called Eurosclerosis and to increase the competitiveness of European manufacturers vis-à-vis their U.S. and Japanese rivals. In this connection, the AFL-CIO is quite justified in pointing out that the socio-economic differentials within the countries of Europe are not nearly as great as those separating the U.S. from Mexico and that the gap between the rich and the poor western European nations is much narrower than the gap between the U.S. and Mexico.

A study published by the National Planning Association examines the different results of European and U.S. labor market policy.[1] Among other things, the study points out that the income situation in Europe has improved greatly over the past 15 years compared to that in the United States. European Community (EC) hourly compensation levels rose from $5 (or 79 percent of the U.S. level) in 1975, to $13 (or 98 percent of the U.S. level) in 1987. By 1990, they had increased to $17 (or 115 percent of the U.S. level). This advance is no accidental result of market forces. European management and labor groups have decided to create a high productivity environment that fosters quality products and a high standard of living.

Although the success of labor market policies in Europe can be compared to the NAFTA market of the future only to a limited degree, the EC policies and the NAFTA do have two things in common. They both represent attempts to find an answer to the increasing globalization of economic activity. They are also both based on the realization that national economic policy alone can no longer provide satisfactory answers to the questions raised by worldwide economic upheavals.

THE EC's SOCIAL DIMENSION

In contrast to the neoliberal policy approach of the NAFTA, European integration has from the outset been accompanied by the attempt to take the social dimension of the single market into consideration. Although European labor representatives complain that economic integration has been given far higher priority than social integration and harmonization, the process of integration in Europe to date can supply insights that may be useful to the NAFTA.

Three central aspects of Europe's social dimension that will be addressed below are the European dialogue, the European Social Fund, and the European Regional Fund. But by way of introduction, it is worth noting that in 1957, the aim of the EC treaty was proclaimed as follows:

> The task of the community is to promote the harmonious development of economic life within the community, the steady and balanced expansion of economic activity, increased stability, and the speedy improvement of the standards of living as well as closer ties between the countries joined together in this community through the establishment of a common market, and the gradual convergence of the economic policies of the member states.

Practical economic policy was primarily aimed at the abolition of tariffs and the elimination of barriers to the free movement of individuals, services, and capital. At that time, the sole social policy instrument was the European Social Fund, which was designed to improve the working and living conditions of European citizens. In connection with the implementation of the social aspects of integration, this fund has gained in significance in recent years.

The Maastricht Treaty is intended to mark a new integration milestone along the road to complete European union. At present, following the delay in ratification in Great Britain, it is not possible to predict with certainty whether unification will be achieved by 1996 or 1999. Alongside the goal of achieving political union, social harmonization will be extended, albeit with the resistance of the British government. It must be noted that the different social policy conceptions of the member states have greatly complicated the process of social union. The active commitment of the European trade unions, which despite central criticism still support the Maastricht Treaty, is largely responsible for the fact that the social dimension of the single market has been able to gain more well-defined contours in recent years.

Following the intervention of the unions, the Social Charter was signed by the heads of government in December 1989. The following are a few of the areas covered by the Charter: improvement of living and working conditions, employment concerns, freedom of coalition and wage negotiations, and equality of the sexes.

Although this Social Charter is not legally binding—a major criticism made by the trade unions—numerous binding guidelines have been in force since the end of the 1970s and have become law in the member states. These laws regulate such things as equal treatment of men and women in employment and equal pay for equal work, as well as various collective protective rights for eventualities such as factory closures and mass dismissals.

European Dialogue

In 1985, direct social dialogue took place between employers' organizations and trade unions. Jacques Delors emphasized that the realization of the single market must be accompanied by the organization and creation of a social European infrastructure. This infrastructure would serve as a cornerstone for social dialogue and negotiations between the employer and the employee organizations on a European level. Several equal representation working groups were created and have drawn up joint statements on important social policy topics. One example is the statement on "Perspectives for a European Labour Market." The authors emphasize that structural policy must be aimed at creating new jobs and that one of the prerequisites for this is painstaking observation of developments on the labor market.

The social dialogue in Europe clearly shows that public discussion is indispensable to the achievement of social policy goals and that the information and consultation rights of employee representatives are absolutely essential to this discussion. The Economic and Social Committee of the EC is of major importance in this regard. The Committee, which has been in existence since 1957, is comprised of three groups representing economic and social life. These groups are employees, trade unions, and so-called different interests, including consumers, professionals, and craftsmen. The Committee enjoys information and consultation rights in all social and economic policy areas and submits statements to the EC Commission on all important measures.

From a European point of view, it was astounding to learn that during the Bush administration, there were no broad-based public discussions in connection with the creation of the NAFTA, particularly in view of the fact that this agreement would have far-reaching consequences for the population of the internal market. Even the information given to the Labor Advisory Committee (LAC) for Negotiations and Trade Policy was totally inadequate. When the agreement was announced on August 12, 1992, copies of a complete draft were not distributed to the LAC. It remains to be seen how committed the Clinton administration will be to the social charter implications of the NAFTA.

However, the social dimensions of such a union cannot be realized in the absence of public discussions that incorporate private citizens, the trade union movement, employees' associations, the consumer federations, and the environmental organizations in the states concerned. Much can be learned in this area from the so-called Fortress Europe.

The European Social Fund

Is the social fund an instrument for common labor market policy? The European structural funds are of special importance regarding the social dimension of the single European market. As early as 1957, the Treaty of Rome contained provisions for the creation of a European social fund to promote further training measures and support the mobility of Europe's unemployed. The initial aim of the original six EC signatories (the Benelux countries, France, Italy, and Germany) was to create a special solution to the Mezzogiorno, an underdeveloped region in southern Italy. Persistent and steadily increasing unemployment has led to an enormous increase in the demands made on the social fund. In 1987 alone, the fund managed $12 billion, approximately 6 percent of the total EC budget.

I believe that a social fund would also be conceivable within the context of the NAFTA for the development of a common labor market policy in the fields of qualifications and training. The rapid pace of structural change, the advance of systemic rationalization concepts, the decreasing significance of the Taylor model of mass production, and the increase in specific intra-company flexible strategies call for well-trained, highly qualified employees who can think creatively and act independently. This applies both to developed countries like the United States and Canada and to newly industrializing countries like Mexico. These developments accentuate the need for cross-border qualification programs similar to those in existence for several years within the framework of the European social fund.

Direct investment within the EC depends to a large extent on the options for opening new production in Spain, Portugal, or Greece and the availability of a well-trained and skilled workforce in these areas. In the future, it will only be possible to build up modern industrial companies with new production concepts that can compete on an international level in North America if a qualified workforce is on hand to do the job. This also applies to service industries, which will have to build up around these companies.

It would therefore be little short of disastrous for the future of the NAFTA if the parties neglected to use further negotiations or the creation of a social fund to set clear signals for common qualification programs. The need for this type of qualification program is nothing new in the United States. The U.S. Department of Labor has already submitted a draft bill entitled "National Youth Apprenticeship Act of 1992" to Congress which points in this direction. A common approach along these lines is also necessary and would prove beneficial within the NAFTA itself.

The necessary improvement of the qualification potential further requires harmonization of incomes and social benefits if systematic distortion of competition is to be avoided in the NAFTA in the long term. The strategy of raising the wage differential within the NAFTA to the sole criterion for direct investment is doomed to failure in the long term from both a social and an ecological point of view.

The European Regional Fund

Finally, is the European regional fund an instrument for the elimination of regional disparities? In contrast to the political approach behind the NAFTA, the EC made an expressed commitment to the elimination of regional disparities and the approximation of the living conditions of its citizens at the outset in the Treaty of Rome. Although income differentials in the EC are lower than in North America, average net earnings still range from $13,000 in Portugal to $50,000 in Luxembourg, a ratio of 1:4. Regional disparities in the area of unemployment are even more pronounced. While 30 percent of Andalusians are without jobs, the unemployment rate in Luxembourg is a mere 2 percent. The expansion of the EC to the south has served to further increase regional disparities. Blind faith in the self-healing powers of the single European market would accentuate these differences even further. Thanks to a 1989 amendment to the Single European Act, the Community has been able to take more effective measures to solve the structural problems of the weaker regions and their disadvantaged inhabitants. The EC Commission describes these disadvantages as follows: inadequate or neglected infrastructure, weak or outdated industrial structures, decline of towns and depopulation, and high unemployment with particularly serious consequences for young Europeans.

The situation reported by the EC Commission hardly differs in its basic findings from the situation in the future North American internal market. In contrast to the NAFTA, however, the EC is pursuing an active structural policy in its attempt to reduce regional disparities. Funds totaling over $119 billion were made available for this purpose between 1989 and 1993. How these funds are disbursed depends on development plans that have yet to be created. In some countries, the important social groups have been incorporated into the preparation of these development plans in an attempt to ensure the necessary social dialogue on this level as well.

CONCLUSION

In the light of experiences in Europe, North American trade unions are to be supported in their view that without the instrument of structural policy, a regional fund, and an environmental and social charter, the free trade agreement will serve only to further deregulate the North American labor market. This deregulation will cut jobs, reduce wages, and curtail the social achievements of employees in all three countries.

Although any comparison between the EC and the future NAFTA will always be incomplete, and though the similarities between the two should not be overemphasized, it can be said with a high degree of certainty that the EC experience shows that the NAFTA must progress beyond the status of pure market integration if it is to be successful as an institution.

Note

1. Richard S. Belous, Rebecca S. Hartley, and Kelly L. McClenahan, eds., *European and American Labor Markets: Different Models and Different Results* (Washington, D.C.: National Planning Association, 1992).

21. *The Role of Nongovernmental Organizations and the NAFTA*

by Cathryn L. Thorup

For the most part, past analyses of the NAFTA have focused less on the socio-political impact of North American integration and more on the economic consequences of the agreement. In this paper, I would like to refocus these discussions and examine the issue of social cohesion.

The NAFTA has contributed to an unprecedented level of transnational networking and coalition-building among grass-roots organizations in North America. This has affected decisions not only in the commercial arena, but in other arenas like the environment and immigration as well. Studying the effects of this networking allows us to differentiate between government and society and helps clarify the notion of "national" interest. This allows us to look beyond the level of public and private sector elites toward new actors within the civil societies of all three countries.

NONGOVERNMENTAL ORGANIZATIONS

During the 1980s, economic and political elites in Mexico City and Washington became well acquainted. Together they negotiated Mexico's debt rescheduling and dueled over Central America. This interaction represented a drastic shift from the 1970s, when such contact was rare. The 1980s, however, saw change, and the 1990s seem destined to continue this transformation. I believe we will see a quantum leap in the level of contact between all three countries, this time, though, at the level of nongovernmental organizations (NGOs).

International relations today bear scant resemblance to earlier models based upon the interaction of unitary rational actors. Nongovernmental groups are working in concert with counterpart organizations around the world, contributing to a transnationalization of civil society.

The significance of this trend for North America became apparent during the NAFTA negotiations in 1990. Cross-border citizen diplomacy clearly influenced the course and outcome of the bargaining over the shape and substance of an integrated North America, making it clear that relations between the United States, Mexico, and Canada were no longer in the exclusive domain of economic and political elites. Two years later, private citizens play an increasingly important role in setting the parameters of the trilateral relationship.

This transnationalization of civic participation entails a dispersion of power to domestic interest groups and cross-border coalitions, curtailing the ability of governments to manage their relations on a strict government-to-government basis. This dispersion of power also sets the stage for a much more complex type of interaction. As a result, in the context of U.S.-Mexican relations, conflict has the potential to become less nationally grounded and more closely linked to class, issue, and sectoral interests.

NEGOTIATING ECONOMIC INTEGRATION

The increasingly dense network of societal interdependence has meant that negotiating economic integration has become more complex, forcing negotiators to take more issues and actors into account. In 1990 and 1991, domestic interest groups not only began meeting with their direct counterparts in Mexico, Canada, and the United States, but also began identifying support within the ranks of groups representing other sectoral interests inside their own country and across borders. Canadian labor interests met not only with U.S. and Mexican labor organizers, but also with agricultural, environmental, and human rights groups.

The original impact of this antifast-track, cross-border network that developed in the early stages of the NAFTA negotiations was threefold. First, it significantly complicated the process of securing fast-track authority for the NAFTA and may still delay final approval by the U.S. Congress of the agreements. Rather than allow immediate acceptance of the agreements, these cross-border groups insisted that their governments give serious consideration to environmental concerns and issues of worker retraining and adjustment. In fact, it is the organizational efforts of these NGOs that must be credited for the current emphasis onenvironmental and labor questions.

Second, the debate over fast track and the NAFTA has served as a common denominator for discussion and action on the part of groups with very different institutional agendas. Cross-border networks and coalitions have served as the cornerstone for the building of an informal network of domestic interest groups and grass-roots constituencies in all three countries. This has enabled the participants to do several things: to view their specific issues, for example, human rights, the environment, or trade, within a broader framework; to network with a variety of groups with whom they would not normally come into contact; to define common areas of concern and explore areas of disagreement; to create public forums of high visibility where they can express their opinions; to explore alternative tactics and strategies for the pursuit of their trade and nontrade objectives with potential political allies; and to identify sources of intellectual and financial support for their efforts.

The third effect of these coalitions is that they have demonstrated the vulnerability of national decisionmakers in the countries involved to nongovernmental organizing. NGO coalitions have quickly and convincingly underscored their potential to disrupt the management of North American relations by policy elites and to force these elites to negotiate for the political support of these cross-border coalitions that can, in fact, act as a wild card. Traditional equations of power may change as the U.S. or Mexican governments begin to side with cross-border coalitions determined to push the NAFTA in particular directions. It is important to balance a vision of these groups as basically destabilizing influences with the recognition that, however, NGOs are weaving together the interests of the citizenry of each of these three countries, thus contributing to the formation of an evolving sense of societal interdependence.

Although private actors have made their presence known in the United States, Mexico, and Canada for years, the type of interaction taking place today has never occurred at such a level of intensity or with such high stakes. The effectiveness of the cross-border groups is enhanced by the extent to which their members recognize the issue linkages between different groups and are able to seek common ground with other like-minded grass-root constituencies. Over time, these new modalities of citizen diplomacy have the potential to challenge traditional asymmetries in the relations between these three countries.

San Diego/Tijuana is the site of the most intense daily interaction between the United States and Mexico. It is in these cities where the costs and benefits of economic integration and the NAFTA's impact on social cohesion will be first and most keenly felt. Unlike the residents of other border areas, such as El Paso/Juarez who have grown up together, many of the people of San Diego remain reluctant to admit that they live on the border. They prefer to view the city as a lovely cul-de-sac rather than an international gateway. In fact, there is a psychological barrier in place between San Diego and Tijuana that far surpasses anything that the INS or U.S. Customs could set up in order to keep these two communities apart. However, blatant racism and public displays of hostility against immigrants have been superseded by a more substantive and sophisticated discussion of the economic burden created by immigrants upon scarce state and county resources. In the context of a severe economic crisis, this serves to further fan community support for greater interdiction efforts. This disjuncture between the costs imposed by immigration and the ability of local communities to respond has provoked rising levels of community tension.

In this context, citizen diplomacy and cross-border networks and coalitions take on particular significance. There are many NGOs in this region that perform both service and advocacy functions vis-à-vis the immigrant community. They do everything from providing health care, legal services, and housing to monitoring the human rights of immigrants. They also serve as interlocutors with U.S. and Mexican public officials and help to fashion the local community response to Mexican immigration. Although these NGOs are based primarily on the U.S. side of the border, there are several key players in Tijuana as well.

In addition to the networking and coalition-building that is taking place at the local level, a series of trinational immigration networks are beginning to take shape. In October 1992 in Reynosa, the Trinational Exchange on Human Rights was established with the participation of about 50 activists from the United States (including representatives from San Diego), Mexico, and Canada.

NGO ORGANIZING AND THE NAFTA

Clearly, the NAFTA continues to provide the common denominator for these exchanges. It is a topic to which all of these groups can relate. Of course, it is also a topic that in some sense divides these groups because they have no general consensus on the NAFTA's value. It is here that we see pronounced differences between Canadian NGOs and their U.S. and Mexican counterparts. The former generally oppose the NAFTA and have very strong cross-sectoral networks and greater group discipline, while the latter have a much more diverse perspective on the NAFTA. It is therefore unclear how long the NAFTA can continue serving as the only catalyst for these discussions.

With the NAFTA negotiations as its foundation, however, a basic network of contacts has been established and a long process of trust-building, information-sharing, and transnational and cross-sectoral networking has begun among groups whose eventual areas of influence will transcend the economic arena. What remains to be determined is how quickly this network will develop and how far it will evolve. It appeared initially as a reaction to a very particular set of circumstances—the pursuit of the NAFTA. It remains to be seen, however, if these cross-border and cross-sectoral coalitions will survive either its approval or its demise.

Ironically, there is some concern among the U.S. and Mexican NGOs that Canadian NGOs will lose interest in coalition-building should the NAFTA be defeated. There are distinct differences in the organizational styles of Canadian, American, and Mexican NGOs at the grass-roots level. There are clear asymmetries of power, representation, organizational capacity, political autonomy, and so forth. Similarly, there is no guarantee of a natural and permanent affinity of interests on all issues. It remains to be seen whether this period of frequent interaction will produce an attenuation of some of these differences.

A key challenge for NGOs will be to institutionalize their networks in order to make themselves more permanent. Traditionally, civil society's capacity to sustain institutions has been weak. That assessment may prove inadequate in the future, however, as grass-roots actors and other nongovernmental players develop new modes of communication, connection, and cooperation. The institutional arrangements they develop may be quite unlike any that are known today. Like the organizations that formed them, these institutional arrangements may be more fluid with shifting parameters. Rather than a building that can be touched, these actors may tap into electronic networks or develop entirely new modes of interaction. The explosion of computer networking has significantly enhanced the organizational capacity of NGOs in other sectors, enabling them to communicate with each other with relative ease and without great expense.

In Mexico, there is an effort to move beyond the discussion of the NAFTA and the economic reform process—to which many of these groups are now basically resigned—to a discussion of other topics such as political opening in Mexico. Although the latter subject is a difficult issue around which to do cross-border organizing—because it is a topic that is less directly germane to non-Mexican NGOs and more closely tied to particular political objectives in Mexico—it has nevertheless begun to spark some interest among non-Mexican NGOs.

The large-scale growth of transnational, multi-sectoral NGO coalitions may have to await the appearance of another overarching issue of interest like the NAFTA that will permit a brokering out of parochial political and social agendas. Because it is precisely this transnational and transsectoral aspect of these coalitions that gives them their strength, this period of transformation is critically important. Although the NAFTA was the spark that created many of them, these transnational entities ultimately must transcend the NAFTA in order to mature institutionally. This will require the resolving the current tensions among potentially competing political and social agendas and organizational asymmetries.

The transnational, transsectoral aspects of nongovernmental networks and coalitions vastly expands the knowledge base, the scope of activities, and the influence of civil society in the United States, Mexico, and Canada. In the process, it weaves together the interests of the citizenry in these three countries and enhances societal interdependence. Long the norm within the public sector and the business world, these connections will serve to empower nongovernmental actors. Over time, cross-border and cross-sectoral organizations promise to add an entirely new dimension to the relationship between state and society, one which ultimately has the potential to alter the balance of power among nations.

National Planning Association

The National Planning Association is an independent, private, nonprofit, nonpolitical organization that carries on research and policy formulation in the public interest. NPA was founded during the Great Depression of the 1930s when conflicts among the major economic groups—business, labor, agriculture—threatened to paralyze national decisionmaking on the critical issues confronting American society. NPA is dedicated to the task of getting these diverse groups to work together to narrow areas of controversy and broaden areas of agreement as well as to map out specific programs for action in the best traditions of a functioning democracy. Such democratic and decentralized planning, NPA believes, involves the development of effective government and private policies and programs not only by official agencies but also through the independent initiative and cooperation of the main private sector groups concerned.

To this end, NPA brings together influential and knowledgeable leaders from business, labor, agriculture, and the applied and academic professions to serve on policy committees. These committees identify emerging problems confronting the nation at home and abroad and seek to develop and agree upon policies and programs for coping with them. The research and writing for these committees are provided by NPA's professional staff and, as required, by outside experts.

In addition, NPA's professional staff undertakes research through its central or "core" program designed to provide data and ideas for policymakers and planners in government and the private sector. These activities include research on national goals and priorities, productivity and economic growth, welfare and dependency problems, employment and human resource needs, and technological change; analyses and forecasts of changing international realities and their implications for U.S. policies; and analyses of important new economic, social and political realities confronting American society.

In developing its staff capabilities, NPA has increasingly emphasized two related qualifications. First is the interdisciplinary knowledge required to understand the complex nature of many real-life problems. Second is the ability to bridge the gap between theoretical or highly technical research and the practical needs of policymakers and planners in government and the private sector.

Through its committees and its core program, NPA addresses a wide range of issues. Not all of the NPA trustees or committee members are in full agreement with all that is contained in these publications unless such endorsement is specifically stated.

For further information, contact:

National Planning Association
1424 16th Street, N.W.
Suite 700
Washington, D.C. 20036

Tel (202) 265-7685
Fax (202) 797-5516

Friedrich Ebert Foundation

The Friedrich Ebert Foundation is a nonprofit, private educational institution, committed to the concepts and basic values of social democracy and the labor movement.

The Friedrich Ebert Foundation functions in the spirit of Friedrich Ebert, the first president of the German republic of 1919-1933. It was by his legacy that the Foundation was established. The worldwide activities of the Foundation memorialize the spirit of Friedrich Ebert—a statesman of democracy.

The aims of the Friedrich Ebert Foundation include:

- political and civic education in a democratic spirit for persons from all walks of life;
- fostering international understanding and partnership with developing countries;
- support through scholarships for exceptionally talented students, young graduate students and young scholars from Germany and abroad;
- scholarly research within the educational institutions of the Foundation in Germany and abroad, as well as support to other academic and scientific facilities; and
- fostering the arts and culture as elements of a living democracy.

Additional facts:

- Headquartered in Bonn, Germany, the Foundation's 767 member staff operates with offices in 74 countries and is actively involved in nearly 250 projects in 110 countries;
- In 1991, the Friedrich Ebert Foundation sponsored 2,200 scholarship holders and hosted nearly 100,000 visitors at educational programs.

For further information contact:

Friedrich Ebert Foundation
Washington Office
1155 15th Street, N.W.
Suite 1100
Washington, D.C. 20005

Tel (202) 331-1819
Fax (202) 331-1837

Institute of the Americas

The Institute of the Americas, an independent, inter-American institution, is devoted to enhancing private sector collaboration and communications as well as political and economic relations between Latin America and the United States and Canada.

Located on the campus of the University of California, San Diego, 30 miles from the border with Mexico, the Institute provides a unique hemispheric perspective on the opportunities opened by dramatic economic and social change in Latin America and in its links to the U.S. and Canada. The Institute's relationship with the University ensures a high caliber of intellectual input and analysis for Institute events and programs.

In addition, the Institute has always been actively involved in the life of San Diego and the border region. The international board and hemisphere-wide corporate membership allows the Institute to play a constructive role in helping define and refine the economic, political and social agenda for reform throughout the region.

The Institute is supported by corporate and individual members who participate in conferences, workshops, and multi-year projects of the Institute. Funding is also provided by generous support from several private international foundations and U.S. government agencies.

Over the years, the agenda of the Institute has coalesced around five broad policy themes: privatization; environment; energy; capital markets; and free trade arrangements. These five program and research areas constitute the bulk of the Institute's work, but are complemented by time-sensitive projects such as border infrastructure financing or information services.

The Institute's 28-member inter-American board includes prominent private sector representatives from throughout the region. The board is chaired by Richard Hojel of Mexico. Amb. Paul H. Boeker has served as president of the Institute since 1988, and Colleen S. Morton has served as vice president since March 1993. The Institute's inter-American staff consists of 12 full-time professionals and a number of Latin American visiting research fellows, part-time employees, graduate student interns, and volunteers.

The Institute also publishes *News & Events* and its flagship periodical *Hemisfile*, a distinctive bimonthly of political and economic trends in the Americas. This highly regarded new publication reaches some 25,000 readers annually.

For further information, contact:

Institute of the Americas
10111 North Torrey Pines Road
La Jolla, CA 92037

Tel (619) 453-5560
(619) 277-0600
Fax (619) 453-2165